The Schizophrenia Complex

Eve Maram

CHIRON PUBLICATIONS • ASHEVILLE, NORTH CAROLINA

www.ChironPublications.com

Interior and cover design by Danijela Mijailovic
Cover art by Eve Maram 1983
Printed primarily in the United States of America.

ISBN 978-1-68503-060-5 paperback
ISBN 978-1-68503-061-2 hardcover
ISBN 978-1-68503-062-9 electronic
ISBN 978-1-68503-063-6 limited edition paperback

Library of Congress Cataloging-in-Publication Data Pending

Be silent and listen: have you recognized your madness and do you admit it? Have you noticed that all your foundations are completely mired in madness? . . . Do you not want to recognize your madness and welcome it in a friendly manner? You wanted to accept everything. So accept madness too. Let the light of your madness shine, and it will suddenly dawn on you. Madness is not to be despised and not to be feared, but instead you should give it life. . . . If you want to find paths, you should also not spurn madness, since it makes up such a great part of your nature. . . . Be glad that you can recognize it, for you will thus avoid becoming its victim. Madness is a special form of the spirit and clings to all teachings and philosophies, but even more to daily life, since life itself is full of craziness and at bottom utterly illogical. Man strives toward reason only so that he can make rules for himself. Life itself has no rules. That is its mystery and its unknown law. What you call knowledge is an attempt to impose something comprehensible on life.

—C. G. Jung, *The Red Book*

Also from Eve Maram:
Psychopathy Within, Chiron Publications

For my mother

Contents

Author's Note

Clinical case histories and stories presented in this text are true, but details have been altered to protect privacy.

Foreword

By Thomas Elsner, J.D., M.A., Jungian Analyst

Dr. Eve Maram's *The Schizophrenia Complex* is not a book about schizophrenia *per se* but about the atmosphere surrounding that psychiatric diagnosis. It is a book about how we understand, feel, experience, and react to schizophrenia and about how that diagnosis affects both those who suffer from the illness and their family members, friends, and loved ones. One can have a schizophrenia complex without having schizophrenia and one can also have schizophrenia without having a schizophrenia complex since the complex is a *conscious* response.

In this respect, Dr. Maram is uniquely qualified to write this book. She is a forensic psychologist and Jungian analyst whose adult son was diagnosed with schizophrenia. In offering this book to the world, she draws not only from her clinical experience and training but even more so from a deep well of lived experience, love, suffering, and hope.

Schizophrenia is not a popular topic. It is a lonely topic. We do not live in a world where it is possible to openly talk about it. Even writing about schizophrenia can carry with it the feeling of being somehow illegitimate in the eyes of normal society, of overstepping boundaries. What will people think? So, it is an act of courage to write with the intention of finding a new way of belonging by embracing the truth but all the while hearing the voices of the *status quo* threatening one with alienation and rejection. Thus, in the very act of writing about schizophrenia, Dr. Maram has experienced and lived through the schizophrenia complex that she eloquently, clearly, with both love and understanding, articulates in this book.

She knows from where she speaks, and that is the reason why her book resonates from the ground up with Eros and with down to earth relevance for all those who are in any way confronting their own, society's, and/or a loved one's experience of schizophrenia. In some ways, Dr. Maram's book invites the reader into relational and soulful contact with what she refers to, following Jung, as "the natural state of the unconscious," and the subjective experience of being pulled into the "night-sea journey."

Archetypal themes resonate throughout this book – eros and chaos, the Great Mother and the Divine Child, order and disorder – out of the depths of a great unsolved, perhaps unsolvable, mystery of our being. Awareness of the archetypal symbolism helps with what is perhaps the main thesis, namely that "the cure for psychopathology is to un-pathologize it" through a depth psychological perspective. Even more so however, even more uniquely, it is Dr. Maram's personal capacity to consciously "go there" and articulate the experience of consciously felt emptiness and dissociative chaos, all the while mixing deep love and compassion into the process.

Acknowledgments

I am profoundly grateful to significant others for the birthing of this book, including:

My family - for your love, support, tolerance, and ultimate generosity of spirit. Special mention to my son, who granted me permission to share a difficult piece of his deeply personal story with the world, toward a greater good.

The following Jungian analysts whose powerful contributions to the gestational process of this work are its foundation. Thank you for your wisdom and guidance:

Marilyn Marshall
Deborah Stewart
Monika Wikman
Steven Zemmelman

Chiron Publications
My expert editor, Sharron Dorr

Preface

Seven years ago—or was it a lifetime?—I had a dream that I am now reminded of as I begin this book on the schizophrenia complex that I put off writing for so long: I was alone in an underground area of a large, unfamiliar building (maybe a YMCA), needing to complete my workout by diving into a small, round, rimmed pool of cold, dark water in the center of a small, windowless, dimly lit room. I was anxious and torn, as I felt that in order to complete what I expected of myself, I needed to dive in and start swimming, but the prospect was terrifying. Even in the dream, although I could not bring myself to actually take the plunge, I could vividly imagine what it would be like to be swimming tight laps in this narrow, black, seemingly bottomless sinkhole—far from the light of day, alone and claustrophobic. At the time, upon reflection, I worried that this dream implied I was less open to my unconscious than I prided myself on being as a good Jungian. What I perceive now is that this was a (necessarily) unsettling, prospective message from my own depths, something far from my conscious attitude and certainly not arriving by choice. That was March, and on July 2, my adult son had an unexpected psychotic break, leaving the rest of us metaphorically doing laps in the darkness, trying to get back on solid ground. In the years since, my journey has involved developing a relationship with schizophrenia and our complexes around it, first through my son, who has blessedly returned from the unreachable depths, and then more recently—as we have all had some time to breathe—through the rest of our family, all of whom love him and are so deeply affected by his trajectory. It is the feeling dimension of this experience which constitutes my focus here. My son did not undergo his deep dive alone. The feelings associated with his journey continue to impact our lives, along with the unsolicited onus of trying to shift forever an unbidden hereditary burden: the previously unspoken complex in our family—generated by the experience of having a family member with schizophrenia. On some level, which I explain more about later, that complex affects families for generations, both literally and psychically.

Introduction

This topic, the schizophrenia complex, struck my soul—demanding my attention. Dealing with its demands has required me to face my fear, denial, resistance, and ultimate not knowing—and undertake this writing anyway. As I have explained in the preface, the topic showed up, unavoidable rather than chosen, inspired by events and circumstances beyond my control that rearranged my life without my permission.

A *complex* is an emotionally charged knot of largely unconscious feelings and beliefs that has a powerful influence on perceptions and behaviors. It is a pod of feeling-toned ideas or images that accumulate around certain *archetypes*, meaning unconscious, universally inherited human patterns of thought or behavior: literal, symbolic, and psychic. At its core, the complex occurs in response to an experience that is in some way archetypal. When complexes are constellated, they are invariably accompanied by affect and remain relatively autonomous. Jung said that a complex "is the image of a certain psychic situation which is strongly accentuated emotionally and is . . . incompatible with the habitual attitude of consciousness."[1] The schizophrenia complex as I conceptualize it, *is not the phenomenon of schizophrenia itself viewed as a complex*, but concerns the emotionally charged thoughts and feelings generated in response to the schizophrenic condition. The archetypal core of such a feeling-toned complex might be the image of chaos.

Seven years ago, what we call *schizophrenia* suddenly meant more to me than I could have anticipated, when it became necessary for me to acknowledge the symptoms of it in my son. He went on an unplanned, night-sea journey into the unconscious, wherein, as is typical in such cases, he lost control of his *ego*— that part of the mind that mediates between the conscious and the unconscious, and is responsible for reality testing and a sense of personal identity. In schizophrenia, the ego becomes flooded with unconscious material, so that the individual's ability to have a conscious sense of self, to navigate reality, and to regulate affect is stymied.

Moreover, we his family were metaphorically pulled into the waves alongside him. The impact of this development on the trajectory of our lives was far reaching, calling upon all of us to adjust to a new reality. For the rest of us in the family, our conscious awareness of the radical change was relatively accessible, although we struggled.

Once my son regained enough ego consolidation to restore his lost affect, he, too, was impacted by the emotional valence of what he had undergone and continues to navigate. During this process, I realized the tremendous power of the emotional effect an encounter with schizophrenia has upon not only the sufferer—once they can feel it—but also upon others. The quality of this encounter with the unconscious is archetypal, and the struggle to cope with such an aspect of our human existence can result in a schizophrenia complex. In other words, *the schizophrenia complex is a subjective experience in response to an archetypal phenomenon.*

My perspective on my family history and my own memories has shifted. How I see the story line of my life— recollections, present awareness, and visions of the future—is now forever altered by my evolving relationship with what we call schizophrenia. Psyche forced me into the process of this writing, and all it evokes in me, amidst a perfect storm of synchronicities.

In this writing, I hold an attitude of curiosity about schizophrenia, pulling at a small representative number of threads from the vast tapestry of writing and thinking about the subject from Jung, Jungians, and many others. However, rather than describing or attempting to define schizophrenia, my focus is to posit the idea of a unique complex that results from our personal and collective attitudes toward it: how its meaning manifests and feels, and the intense emotional response it arouses. The identified sufferer impacts a whole host of others. Conversely, our held attitudes about, and reactions to, schizophrenia also affect those we label as suffering it— potentially arousing their own powerful feelings about the state in which they find themselves, if and once they do. Encounters with schizophrenia inevitably raise the question of how we relate to our own schizophrenic propensities—or at least our dreaded potential thereof—our fears about becoming unmoored. That affective response to a schizophrenic condition can be overwhelming and deeply disturbing, which in itself can generate a unique complex.

In this book, I am focusing on the phenomenological, qualitative aspect of the schizophrenia complex as I conceptualize it. This approach is distinctly different from a causal emphasis and does not posit a theory per se or a systematic approach to clinical practice with schizophrenic clients. Rather, we will explore the feelings and emotions generated by encountering the chaos of madness, from the personal to the collective and archetypal. Madness is archetypal. What topic could be bigger in the psyche than madness? Could it even be a passport to individuation? Here we will be exploring madness and the fear of madness as opposed to the actual psychiatric diagnosis, which takes many forms. Schizophrenia is a diagnostic category as we conceptualize it in Western civilization. The condition of what we call schizophrenia is a variegated phenomenon; psychosis is its hallmark symptom. For the purposes of this writing, when I refer to what we call *schizophrenia*, I am referring to the experience of psychosis to whatever degree it occurs—a radical breakdown of the boundaries of ego consciousness by the unfettered flood waters of the unconscious.

We humans inherently harbor a deep need to feel and believe that things somehow make sense. Owning the searing guilt of self-blame and taking responsibility for painful conditions and circumstances is generally preferable to accepting the unpredictable, often irrational and random nature of our existence. Nonetheless, uncharted, unfair things happen over which we have no control—and we are collectively and personally unceasing in our strategies to deny or avoid the arbitrary reality of such turns of fate. Applying this human proclivity to our attitudes toward schizophrenia, if we reduce it to a disease with a cause we understand and a clear list of consistent symptoms and possible outcomes, even horrible ones—provided both are predictable and inevitable—then we shore up our defenses against the possibility that there are far less logical, less foreseeable factors at play.

This deep-seated set of forces helps to explain our collective resistance to recognizing that individuals diagnosed with this disease can present in incredibly different ways—and that they *can* change, sometimes remarkably. We would generally prefer not to acknowledge the severity of a psychosis, but once the condition is diagnosed, even a negative conclusion is often preferred to an unclear one.

On the other hand, we also resist the idea that improvement is possible, for allowing hope also makes us vulnerable to disappointment. These are defensive attitudes springing from the same motivation: to protect ourselves from uncertainty at all costs. We require definitive answers about schizophrenia when there are few, if any. We crave knowing what to expect when faced with its innate unpredictability. In addition, maintaining a rigid boundary between "us" and "them" ostensibly allows us to disavow our own innate irrationality and potential for psychosis.

Although I refer primarily to my relationship with my son throughout the telling of this story, many other influences are also of vital relevance and significance, including his relationship with his father—the role of the masculine—and his relationships with his younger sister and other family members. Each of these factors holds tremendous personal and archetypal import, not all of which is explored here.

The archetypal story inherently overarches any personal one, including our experience of the schizophrenia complex. Archetypal images offer us the opportunity to recognize and name universal themes in our unique subjective experiences. When and why we recognize ourselves through the frame of a particular myth or archetypal image can be viewed as a synchronistic gift from psyche. The right myth or image at the right time can be a lifesaver. Sometimes archetypal images fit a particular experience, and sometimes they may have more general resonance throughout one's life, across circumstances. For example, the archetypal image of Eros, the god of relatedness, is and has always been my prevailing soul saver in times of crisis: my psychopomp, an inner guide, a mediator between consciousness and the unconscious.

As I have suggested, it seems to me that the archetypal image that best epitomizes the ur-phenomenon of madness, including schizophrenia, is that of Chaos. What we call schizophrenia can be conceptualized in terms of the juxtaposition of the archetypal constructs of chaos and order (when chaos wins). The individual with schizophrenia has had their ego eroded by a flood of archetypal contents: an experience of inner chaos lacking the ordering function of an organizing ego complex.* An encounter with someone in that state generates our own mirroring chaos, calling upon our own potentially overwhelming fears of falling apart. This emotional experience can become what I am defining as a schizophrenia complex.

The emotional ramifications of encountering madness personally or even collectively take many forms. Archetypes are inherently universal to humankind, but the particular archetypal images that correspond to any one human's experience of what we call schizophrenia are unique and intensely personal. In this writing, I refer to the archetypal images of the Great Mother and the Divine Child cautiously. Certainly, dimensions of these particular images have resonated for me personally in my felt experience with my son—but I use these terms guardedly because the scope of their meaning so far exceeds my simplistic description of their application with reference to our relationship.

The archetype of the Great Mother, the personification of the feminine principle, can be broadly defined as *everything*, although her many manifestations include the personal mother, positive and negative. She represents the fertile womb out of

---

* Given that Jung defined *complex* as an "image . . . incompatible with the habitual attitude of consciousness" (p. 1), and given that he inextricably links the ego to consciousness, the concept of an *ego complex* would seem to be a contradiction in terms. Yet, in his quirky, brilliant way, Jung did indeed develop the theory of an ego complex. See my discussion in chapter 1, p. 29.

which all life comes and the darkness of the grave to which it returns. Her fundamental attributes are the capacity to nourish and also to devour. She corresponds to Mother Nature in the primordial swamp. The Great Mother can nourish us, and she can engulf us. In psychological terms, she corresponds to the unconscious, which can nourish and support the ego, or consume it.[2] I imagine this archetype as the vast, feminine, fertile unconscious: an undifferentiated, diffuse, creative ocean of generative possibilities. To be identified with her can take many forms. I am humbled by the magnitude of her mystery, from which I borrow an infinitesimal amount for personal use. My experience of her, as I discuss it here, had to do with feeling unrealistically capable of fixing everything, including my son. I think this archetypal identification on my part was potentially overwhelming to us both. Part of dealing with my schizophrenia complex has involved disidentifying with the Great Mother.

The Divine or Golden Child is an archetypal image of perfection and promise. The Divine Child archetype is associated with qualities of innocence, purity, possibility, and redemption. If properly nurtured, the Divine Child will develop into a "king." Erich Neumann refers to the Divine Child as "a very special son . . . the luminous son."[3] The attention inevitably drawn by this wondrous character has mutual benefits, enabling the Divine Child to flourish but also bringing to the parent figure (often the mother) a sense of pride and achievement too. There is a natural pairing in this regard between the archetypal mother-and-son images, beautifully described by Neumann: "Her luminous aspect, the fruit of her transformative process, becomes the . . . divine spirit-son. . . . Thus the woman experiences her power to bring forth light and spirit."[4] In my case, my son was my first born and only son, onto whom many of my projections automatically moved. I only noticed them and my role in this (unrealistic) set of expectations when he radically departed from the script.

In short, my relationship with my son was heavily informed by the Great Mother and Divine Child archetypes. This was always true, upon reflection, although I became most aware of my archetypal identification when faced with a crisis of faith in the fantasy. These archetypal images continued to infuse my personal experience with my son as he dove deep into the unconscious, until acknowledging this reality became unavoidable and the images could no longer hold. I felt panic, sorrow, and then life-changing humility—and was forced to withdraw my faith in my (mis)perceived power over our story line and my idealized image of us both. I was less concerned with chaos than I was with loss and grieving; less filled with anger, guilt, or shame than with anxiety and sadness. Disidentification with an archetype, while potentially liberating, can feel like an aching loss. I missed the son I thought I knew and the person I used to be, back when I had a sense of Great Mother omnipotence, of magical control over the unfolding of a script laid deep in my soul from before I could remember.

The archetype of Eros was constellated as well. Eros, the god of love writ large, of divine relatedness, transcends logic and offers a wink when harsh circumstances invite despair. As Jung stated in *The Red Book*, "Eros does not tend toward . . . the side of consciousness, conscious will and conscious choice, but toward the side of the heart."[5] This is the precious, positive side of the irrational, divine mystery of our lives: the spark of hope that endures when facing circumstances beyond our control and twists of fate that render us powerless and bereft.

Certainly, archetypally the father—masculine energy— also constitutes an important piece of the overall constellation of my son's experience. While the father role and its meaning are not amplified here, the masculine is addressed in chapter 7 from an archetypal perspective. I will explore this role through the lens of the ancient Mesopotamian god Marduk—the forceful bringer of organization, order, and discriminating action—who tames the chaos of the dark Great Mother, Tiamat, in the context of the Babylonian creation myth, the *Enuma Elish*. I find myself calling upon my inner Marduk—a masculine (animus) ordering function—during the process of this writing in an attempt to reel in the sometimes unwieldy-feeling scope of all I am trying to draw from in my effort to genuinely serve the Muses and stay true to my subject.

Although the following exploration of the schizophrenia complex has deep roots in my personal experience, it by no means ends there. Throughout, I will bridge back and forth between my own story and other material that will set this exploration in a larger context.

The unavoidable truth—that my son has schizophrenia— finally hit me like a thunderbolt after eight years of firmly entrenched denial. Unlike my psychologist husband and me, our daughter refused to collude with our story line of denial; but we persevered with our blinders firmly intact—until that was no longer possible.

Following a first brief spin into psychosis and an even briefer hospitalization at age twenty-two, our beautiful son was sufficiently (over)medicated to function well at work and school for eight years—and graduated from college with a degree in Human Services. Other than being somewhat socially reclusive, he functioned well enough to preserve our denial and maintain our idealized beliefs about our family. My husband and I came up with a convenient, airtight diagnosis: our son had simply suffered an "adjustment disorder with depression and anxiety, with psychotic features." That "worked" until without warning he made a literal, radical departure: he left his job in the family business (a psychological treatment program) at the end of a routine work day—and disappeared. Within twenty-four hours, we discovered that he had simultaneously just as suddenly abandoned his apartment, leaving behind his phone, clothes, and belongings. Soon afterward, it became clear that he had followed a private clarion call to Venice Beach—an infamous, Southern-California beach haven for the homeless, drug addicted, and mentally ill.

Perhaps he was the only homeless individual with an SUV, a 401K, and a medical-insurance plan maintained by his family an hour away in Orange County—or perhaps not. Venice Beach is a California blend of Tijuana and Coney Island, with music thumping and blaring, and a potpourri of motley street vendors, artists, chaos, and blazing sunshine. During my many visits there to visit my son in this unique milieu, I spotted many young people, mostly male, wild-eyed and sunburned, clothes ragged, pacing and loping, gazing skyward, muttering incoherently. Goethe's words come to mind: "Troubled guests on a dark earth."[6] It was heartbreaking to witness and, for me, inseparable from the grim reality that these individuals also surely had mothers somewhere—fathers and, perhaps, siblings somewhere—from whom they had become harshly severed, along with all that ever bound them to whatever former lives they had led. Now they were floating away into some infinite inner space perhaps never to return—lone astronauts spinning through the darkness of the unconscious without a cord to the mothership. Someone had birthed them; likely at some point someone had loved them. During those crazy months, I suppose I, too, felt untethered, floundering around trying to find ground in an impossible, unanticipated, unplanned, terrifying, often unbelievable reality.

There are many memories, scenes, and images to which I can still relate only as a fuzzy, disjointed panoply that arises from the depths of the psyche, bidden or not, through dreams, in an awake state, or in between, curious and compelling—as though recorded by someone else when I was not looking. I now understand the meaning of that whole period in a broader context: coming to terms with life as it is and not how I thought it would or should be.

Years after the crisis was hot, dragged by necessity, I now hold a different attitude and perspective about schizophrenia in general—as well as our personal experience with it. I had to open to this shift in attitude because of how schizophrenia affected my son. My unconditional love for him has always been stronger than fear, and that relational pull—the ever-presence of Eros— withstood the storm of this dark journey. My son has an unusual degree of clear memory and insight about his journey, and has actually written a chronological journal detailing his descent to the deep end of the unconscious and back. Periodically I quote him throughout this book; all quotes are with his permission.

I have deliberately chosen to avoid taking on the monumental and sticky topic of defining schizophrenia and hope to maintain that boundary. That being said, some discussion of what schizophrenia is (or might be) has felt inevitable and necessary, in part because I am convinced that what we have are many interesting theories and no definitive answer. That state of not knowing makes a difference in terms of describing a complex in response to it—which is why I include some mention of its definition and of the theories about it, not as a second main topic, but as context.

What we call *schizophrenia* ultimately describes a relationship with the unconscious. We have no way of knowing what is truly at its core. What we have are beliefs only. Validation of our very existence resides in the mind/brain, so of course there is a neurological contribution to this phenomenon. Neurology can identify the brain processes that accompany the symptoms, but cannot definitively explain the genesis of the brain symptoms. Scientists believe they know, but what they know is incomplete. Biological, psychological, and environmental factors appear evident. From a Jungian perspective, there is also a fundamental archetypal component to this phenomenon. The cause and definition of schizophrenia are ultimately complex and mysterious. C. G. Jung's *The Red Book* represents the quintessence of this broad perspective. Jung's great mind and spiritual tenacity allowed him to enter the vast reaches of his own unconscious—and the still deeper realm of the collective unconscious—while retaining the consciousness necessary to dialogue with and describe his journey, through prolific writing and illustration. Most of us could not possibly engage so intimately with our own "madness" and return intact to tell the story as he does in *The Red Book*.

As I stated in the article, "Dialoguing with My Demon":

I have come to perceive schizophrenia as less about a split mind, as the etymology suggests, than an unruly expanded one. The visions and dreams, the lack of differentiation between the dream world and the waking one that characterize schizophrenia, reflect the diffuse vastness of the unconscious unfettered by the constraints—and the organizing functions—of consciousness. . . .

12

The unconscious as a construct both repels and lures us. Schizophrenia generally just repels us. It represents unconsciousness unbounded, lost in space, a separation of the mind while the body is eerily still before us, staring at or through us from that other intangible dimension on the street corner, strolling lopsidedly down Venice Beach, sleeping on cardboard, in the hospital waiting room, the therapy office—or our living room. Who would face or even visit such a monster voluntarily? After all, that monster represents the aspects of ourselves we would most like to avoid— our own capacity for madness, the mad state of our limited existence, the universal human reality of our eventual absorption into death—the great unsolvable mystery of our very being.[7]

Schizophrenia is described in current clinical psychiatry as a constellation of signs and symptoms that may include hallucinations, delusions, disorganized thinking, and grossly disorganized or abnormal motor behavior, including catatonia. These are referred to as "positive" symptoms because they are feelings and behaviors that are overt, observable, and atypical of the individual's normal functioning. The condition also includes "negative" symptoms that represent a reduction or loss of "normal" functioning in some way: blunting of affect, poverty of speech and thought, apathy, anhedonia (joylessness), lack of social drive or interest, avolition (lost motivation), and inattention to input from the external world.[8] Such negative symptoms are just as compromising and prevalent as positive ones, but are less likely to be noticed by others. Both positive and negative symptoms comprise opposite extremes of abnormal intensity; they are not mutually exclusive but overlap, coexist, and change over time and with medication.

Furthermore, there are several generally recognized sub-types of schizophrenia—paranoid, catatonic, and undifferentiated or hebephrenic (childlike)—although the current *Diagnostic and Statistical Manual of Mental Disorders* (DSM-5-TR) no longer includes these categorial distinctions.

Some types of symptoms show more than others, but a commonality is the inner chaos experienced by someone with an ego submerged in the unconscious. One way this chaos manifests, is in the form of unregulated affect or behavior that may be extraverted, introverted, or both. This characteristic is particularly relevant to the schizophrenia complex, since it is usually the odd behavior reflective of inner chaos that triggers a strong emotional response in those who encounter it.

Psychiatric descriptions of symptoms and how they appear (or do not appear) help us to understand the phenomenon of schizophrenia, but they do not explain its archetypal scope or the aspects of it that are as inherently insoluble as the unconscious itself. They do not explain how it feels to reenter the "real" world from the depths, nor do they address what happens to others who encounter the disturbing symptoms in a loved one—or a stranger. Those feeling dimensions are the realm of the schizophrenia complex as I am defining it here, and the focus of this writing: the affective experience of the person with schizophrenia, or of those impacted, and whether those feelings can be conscious or not. All that being said, there are extreme differences in what we mean when we use the term *schizophrenia*, in part due to the wide variations in how this anomaly manifests.

Like most things we would prefer to avoid, we opt for definitive explanations and solutions; but realistically there is an incredible, unpredictable, unchartable array of combinations of different personality characteristics that result in an even greater multitude of ways to be what we call *schizophrenic*. In the end, the mix is what matters most: from the creative-genius type (such as the brilliant mathematician John Nash, subject of the book and subsequent movie, *A Beautiful Mind*); to the International Hearing Voices Network (yes, there is such a group, clearly the extraverted branch); to those who can function well, hold jobs, and have relationships; to those who cannot hold anything, stay anywhere, or sustain existence in the conscious world at all. We can medicate the symptoms that make it impossible for an individual to function in society, but managing the illness overall remains an unresolved challenge.

Probably an even greater challenge than the clinical details is the prevailing collective fear that erodes any remediating efforts and poisons reentry for an individual so marked. Many who suffer this disease, like my son, had successful, healthy, normal lives into young adulthood, only to hear the unbidden call of the unconscious and guilelessly enter an unanticipated dimension, leaving their families and friends, jobs, possessions, and established homes untethered. Cancer and diabetes invoke our sympathetic response. Not so schizophrenia, although the fallout from this illness and the havoc it can wreak on an individual's life—and upon those closest to them—is as real as acute physical ailments. Our fear of schizophrenia reflects our deep fear of the unconscious.

Media culture defines what is happy, normal, and desirable with increased intensity since the advent of Facebook, Instagram, Twitter, and other widely accessible forms of impression management. In such a context, the pull toward individuation and developing a relationship with the unconscious is perhaps less congruous than ever, although throughout history—certainly in Jung's time—such ideas have never been collectively popular. Today, the pressure is incredibly high to conform to the image of "normal," to seek and display what media culture portrays as successful.

In stark contrast, schizophrenia is an unwanted, visual, visceral reminder of those aspects of ourselves that we fear, abhor, and would prefer to deny: aspects that threaten to make us feel weird, out of control, different, unpopular, and "crazy." Schizophrenia represents the epitome of the "not me," perhaps even beyond the shadow and potentially more terrifying: all that we do not know and would desperately avoid. It is that which is alien to ego consciousness—the true "otherness" within me and in the world.

Viewed in terms of the complex it generates, what does the phenomenon of schizophrenia represent? At the base of this complex, what might be its archetypal core? Resident of the collective unconscious as are all archetypes, it might show up as different symbols and images in myths, fairy tales, and dreams. What happens to us as we encounter this archetypal energy within us personally? Those effects differ as vastly as the many ways to have and be impacted by schizophrenia.

My analyst recently drew my attention to a collection of essays edited by Jungian analyst Murray Stein, *Mad Parts of Sane People in Analysis*. What about *Sane Parts of Mad People in Analysis*? Or *Mad Parts of Sane Analysts*? Is sanity—or madness—really a consistently definable demarcation? Apparently, I have more questions than answers, but I have a strong hunch that being human bridges both. Certainly, in the process of analysis a meaningful encounter with any "mad parts" in our analysands inevitably calls upon our own murky depths, making for a shared experience that is qualitatively fundamental to the therapeutic alliance. As a clinician, my own ego's relationship to the unconscious, my own felt attitude and emotional response to madness—my schizophrenia complex—affects how I respond to a client suffering psychosis. In *Mad Parts*, Nathan Schwartz-Salant's essay notes the following:

> Speaking about a psychotic part is, in a sense, a contradiction. . . . Psychotic states, like the waters of chaos in alchemy or in creation myths, are psychic spaces in which Cartesian language fails. These states readily extend to the analyst, creating a field in which it is not possible to state who is containing the "psychotic part." Rather, one deals with a field phenomenon that cannot be reduced to separable structures.[9]

Our relationship with our inner "madness"—with the unconscious—has everything to do with what schizophrenia means in our culture and in our psyches, both personal and collective. Individually and collectively, our avoidance of this aspect of human existence is significant. Fear, avoidance, and blind hatred—"othering"—create a marginalization that damages at least as deeply as a scattered mind, if not more so. It is a painful reality that for some people bearing the diagnosis, the reactions of people around them are more distressing than the condition itself. Inevitably, caring others around such an individual are affected by stigmatizing attitudes toward the condition. In the final analysis, our collective and personal revulsion for our own irrational aspects is perhaps the primary illness, the manifestation and projection of which is carried by those among us who, due to ill fate or genetics or both, have no choice but to be more fully drafted into the deep zones of the unconscious than the rest of us. These unwitting warriors manifest an archetypal image of alienation, and their victories are too rarely understood or acknowledged.

The perspective presented here may inspire theories about the schizophrenia complex and concomitant strategies for clinical practice, but that is less my goal than to tell you a story about how I came up with this idea. In our creative efforts to understand (and control) even the most mysterious aspects of our existence, theorizing is inevitable—in part because theories can bind our anxiety about not knowing. The word *theory* means contemplation of the nature of things, derived from the Greek *theoria*, "to look at." The potential downside of an emphasis upon theories is that they can lure us away from our genuine, immediate experience—including with patients—into the safety of dogma. As Jung stated, with implications regarding both theory and practice:

> Every psychotherapist not only has his own method—he himself is that method. . . .
> Theories are to be avoided, except as mere auxiliaries. As soon as dogma is made of them, it is evident that an inner doubt is being stifled.[10]

I hold a contemplative and respectful attitude toward theoria.

To give a sense of the overall conceptual arc of this writing, we will begin with exploring Jung's definition of a schizophrenia complex and comparing it to mine. I will proceed from there to share stories of my own previously hidden family history with schizophrenia—with its generational echoes—and how that influenced my thinking about a schizophrenia complex. Chapter 3 focuses on the phenomenon of schizophrenia as an understandable trigger for terror, particularly given our estranged collective relationship with the unconscious. In chapter 4, I discuss Jung's iconic work with schizophrenia and how it deeply influenced his thinking. Chapter 5 discusses the broad spectrum of theories about the illness and how they have influenced our thinking and emotional responses over decades. Chapter 6 introduces alchemical implications of our understanding of schizophrenia and our responses to it. In chapter 7, we will visit a mythological perspective on the essence of schizophrenia and our attitudes toward it, in the archetypal interplay between chaos and order. Chapter 8 brings us to the role and result of psychotropic medication and the regulation of affect. Chapter 9 introduces yet another lens through which to view schizophrenia and its associated complex: the fairy tale of *The Three Billy Goats Gruff*. Chapter 10 returns us to the real world, offering case examples of therapeutic encounters with clients who have the diagnosis—including discussion about working with this phenomenon and all it constellates in the analyst. In conclusion, chapter 11 emphasizes the archetypal roots of the schizophrenia complex and the central role of Eros in its depotentiation.

This exploration is essentially descriptive, leaving space for curiosity about schizophrenia from various perspectives—including personal, collective, and archetypal—with an emphasis on its many emotional ramifications, which are the realm of the schizophrenia complex. Such an endeavor necessitates some discussion of established theoretical perspectives about schizophrenia and about the schizophrenia complex as Jung defined it, which follows in chapter 5. However, for the overall purposes of this writing, while I value and respect the vast research on this topic, the surface of which I can barely scratch here, I include this discussion as context and am ultimately less concerned with reporting from these perspectives than with staying true to my own. I hope to emphasize the following:

- The schizophrenia complex is both intimately subjective and archetypal, affecting everyone differently.
- The experience of all that we mean by *schizophrenia* and our encounters with it can be conceptualized as the ego's submergence in the unconscious. This is beautifully illustrated by Edward Edinger as quoted in chapter 6.
- The schizophrenia complex can be understood in terms of a profound ripple effect, from the personal to the collective, the numinous, and the symbolic.

Dread surrounds the topic of schizophrenia and anything associated with it. Our often visceral, passionate attitudes about schizophrenia—our emotional responses to madness and chaos—form the archetypal core of what I conceptualize as the schizophrenia complex. I choose to face the dread and indulge my curiosity about the phenomenon. I invite you to join me.

What Is a Schizophrenia Complex?

C. G. Jung described that complexes in schizophrenia—in contrast to those in neurotic disorders—are so radically dissociated from ego that they cannot be integrated into consciousness, or can only reach consciousness at all with the remission of the psychosis "like a mirror broken up into splinters."[1] He writes, "A neurosis . . . is characterized by the relative autonomy of its complexes, but in schizophrenia the complexes have become disconnected and autonomous fragments."[2] This definition of a schizophrenia complex differs from other, feeling-toned complexes. The degree to which a complex is feeling toned as opposed to cut off and compartmentalized from ego consciousness reflects the difference between contents that are neurotic (accessible) and psychotic (split off and dissociated).

According to Jung, complexes can span from normal to psychotic, depending on the degree of incompatibility with our egoic identity. A "normal" complex would involve affective material that is relatively accessible and not completely disconnected from one's awareness. A complex in an individual with schizophrenia would be autonomous to the utmost:

To have complexes is in itself normal; but if the complexes are incompatible, that part of the personality which is too contrary to the conscious part becomes split off. If the split reaches the organic structure, the dissociation is a psychosis, a schizophrenic condition, as the term denotes. Each complex then lives an existence of its own, with no personality left to tie them together.[3]

As Jungian analyst Daryl Sharp explained, "Jung believed that many psychoses, and particularly schizophrenia, were psychogenic, resulting from an *abaissement du niveau mental* [French: a lowering of consciousness] and an ego too weak to resist the onslaught of unconscious contents."[4]

Metaphorically drowning in a schizophrenia complex—where the ego is engulfed in the unconscious—would thus be an extreme example of Jung's timeless quote about how rather than we having our complexes, "our complexes have us."[5]

Psychotic fragmentation implies absolute disconnection from the ego and from conscious feelings and emotions. The complex of an individual with schizophrenia, as Jung described it, is radically dissociated from any unifying personality, a split that reaches the organic structure of the individual. This condition differs from Jung's definition of a complex in general as "feeling-toned," as follows:

It is the *image* of a certain situation which is strongly accentuated emotionally and is, moreover, incompatible with the habitual attitude of consciousness. This image has a powerful inner coherence, it has its own wholeness and, in

WHAT IS A SCHIZOPHRENIA COMPLEX?

addition, a relatively high degree of autonomy, so that it is subject to the control of the conscious mind to only a limited extent, and therefore behaves like an animated foreign body in the sphere of consciousness.[6]

That is, whereas he describes most complexes as knots of incompatible emotions that differ from one's ego syntonic persona—relatively unconscious but accessible to ego consciousness—his definition of a schizophrenia complex is qualitatively different in its characteristic of extreme dissociation from ego consciousness.

Hence, Jung seemed to refer to a schizophrenia complex as the state of schizophrenia itself within an individual bearing its symptoms, rather than an emotional reaction to the condition involving unresolved feelings and beliefs. If having a schizophrenia complex is synonymous with having schizophrenia, then there is no continuum involved in the definition, no gradated spectrum of consciousness; one is either in a state of psychotic dissociation or not. Jung's definition of a schizophrenia complex describes the extreme dissociation from ego consciousness that characterizes the psychotic end of the spectrum.

The late Jungian analyst Erel Shalit discussed the complex as having a task "to serve as a vehicle and vessel of transformation, whereby the archetypal essence is brought into living reality."[7] In someone with a strong enough ego, this process can occur fairly readily: "The complexes enable a relatively smooth transition from the archetypal to the personal."[8] However, for someone in a psychotic state, archetypal contents flood the ego to such an extent that the vessel of transformation cannot hold.

As illustration, Shalit referred to Jung's distinction between "soul complexes" and "spirit complexes,"[9]—the former being more like a "regular," feeling-toned complex and the latter being more like Jung's description of a schizophrenia complex, i.e., radically disconnected from ego consciousness.[10] Jung compared the experience of these two kinds of complexes with the primitive belief in souls and spirits: "Souls correspond to the autonomous complexes of the personal unconscious, and spirits to those of the collective unconscious."[11]

Thus, we may deduce that *soul complexes* are essentially useful to the individual's developing sense of identity since they can be assimilated into consciousness, whereas *spirit complexes* are associated with psychosis—with an ego too weak to withstand the archetypal world, and so the complex cannot perform its transformative task. This differentiation helps to explain Jung's ideas about the differences between feeling-toned complexes (soul complexes) and what he calls a schizophrenia complex (a spirit complex). Jung did not discuss complexes that arise in response to encountering schizophrenia in another person or complexes in people with schizophrenia that are feeling toned and not fully split off.

With that understanding, I am defining a "schizophrenia complex" as a feeling-toned complex in response to an encounter with what we call schizophrenia. Like other feeling-toned complexes, such a complex is only relatively compartmentalized; it is not entirely dissociated, but rather is relatively accessible to consciousness. As I use the term *schizophrenia complex*, it could pertain either to someone responding to an individual with schizophrenia or to someone with schizophrenia who realizes the emotional import of their experience once they recover sufficient ego consolidation to do so.

How to best use Jung's theory of complexes in the context of all we now know—and still do not know—about schizophrenia is an evolving puzzle for me. Jung's thinking can still richly inform our perspective a century later. Consider the following:

> [In schizophrenia] the split-off figures assume banal, grotesque, or highly exaggerated names and characters, and are often objectionable in many other ways. They do not, moreover, co-operate with the patient's consciousness. They are not tactful and they have no respect for sentimental values. On the contrary, they break in and make a disturbance at any time, they torment the ego in a hundred ways; all are objectionable and shocking, either in their noisy and impertinent behaviour or in their grotesque cruelty and obscenity. There is an apparent chaos of incoherent visions, voices, and characters, all of an overwhelmingly strange and incomprehensible nature.[12]

Jung also described what such visitations might ask of someone. He wrote,

> A complex can be really overcome only if it is lived out to the full. In other words, if we are to develop further we have to draw to us and drink down to the very dregs what, because of our complexes, we have held at a distance.[13]

Schizophrenia is beyond deeply frightening. A schizophrenia complex as Jung defined it would be a daunting one to "live out to the full" in order to overcome it. This perhaps reflects the broad disparity between what Jung meant when he refers to the kinds of complexes "normal" and "neurotic" people have, compared with the radically autonomous, dissociated complexes of individuals who have what he called schizophrenia. Such individuals would neither be egoically capable nor inclined to "draw . . . and drink down to the very dregs" what, because of such a complex, they have "held at a distance."

Jung did not address the idea of individuals who do *not* have schizophrenia as having a "schizophrenia complex." We can reasonably conjecture that if such nonpsychotic individuals were to be impacted by a schizophrenia complex as Jung defined one, it would appear healthy and life-affirming *not* to "drink it down to the very dregs."

I do not make the distinction Jung did between the schizophrenia complex characteristic of someone with schizophrenia and the "normal" or "neurotic" complexes of others impacted by the condition, which I also refer to as a schizophrenia complex. The barely accessible unresolved feelings and beliefs we hold about any encounter with madness, even a personal one, are often at least as devastating a challenge as the experience itself.

The Schizophrenia Complex Reconsidered

Schizophrenia itself is not a complex. What we call schizophrenia involves incursions from the unconscious, affective and energic experience disconnected from consciousness. In contrast, the schizophrenia complex as I am describing it has to do with the thoughts and emotions that arise from a *conscious* experience of encountering schizophrenia. Thus, the complex can occur in an individual who has suffered psychosis themselves and recovered

WHAT IS A SCHIZOPHRENIA COMPLEX?

enough ego consciousness to recall, reflect upon, and retrieve ego-associated affect with some insight. The complex is also triggered in others whose lives are impacted by those who suffer schizophrenia. The ramifications of schizophrenia range from intensely personal to collective: family, loved ones, community, and the world at large.

By definition, while in a psychotic state an individual is unable to be ego identified with their experience and thus may not be aware of any suffering at all until the metaphorical spaceship reenters planet Earth with a crash—usually via medication. Those closest to the person inevitably encounter schizophrenia by proxy at a deep level but with their own ego consciousness intact—meaning that, for them, awareness of their loved one's severance from reality is obvious, in addition to grieving the loss of the familiar relationship and reciprocity. That traumatizing realization for family members triggers its own kind of schizophrenia complex—a shocking, unchosen shove into a dimension of human experience most are neither prepared for nor capable of processing with understanding. This promotes a sense of otherness, heightened anxiety, and skittishness about the ability to trust one's own perceptions. ("After all," the thinking goes, "if it can happen to . . . why not me?") The old reality has been forever altered. The new one is confusing at best, unpredictable, and, above all, unknown.

When we witness someone in a psychotic state, the typical reaction is visceral fear and avoidance. The affect and appearance of the psychotic individual is usually strange. On a conscious level, we are repelled by and wary of the oddness. Perhaps on a deeper level, we are frightened by the image of madness unleashed because something in us recognizes it. Even though we do not ourselves consciously understand or speak the language of madness, it is both alien and familiar. Probably even more than the oddness, the whiff of familiarity freaks us out and evokes all our defenses.

For better or worse, schizophrenia is an inscrutable phenomenon that transcends scientific explanation. So, like most things limitless and inexplicable, we are especially desperate to make rational sense of it, to achieve some sense of control. In an Alice in Wonderland-like way, however, it may be that the best way to approach this enigma of human existence—to depotentiate one's own schizophrenia complex—is to look less directly at it, to soften our lenses, and simply to regard and accept the mystery. As the Mad Hatter from *Batman* once explained, trying to understand madness with logic is "not unlike searching for darkness with a torch."[14]

As I have stated, I have always thought of a complex as a knot of unconscious feelings and beliefs that has a powerful influence on perceptions and behaviors; in this case, we are discussing archetypal schizophrenic imagery in the psyche. We might experience such an unconscious pod of feelings and beliefs in images of inner confusion or ego dissociation—chaos, writ large—as I say more about later. This is the fear of ultimate nonbeing, in the sense of complete annihilation, which is different from the fear of death. If one believes in an afterlife of some sort, a heaven above or an astral realm where the spirit might soar, the understanding of death intimates that in some regard the "I" that I have lived will continue on, even if only philosophically or in memory. Maybe not so bad. But *complete annihilation?!*

When we are in the grip of a complex, we may be unaware of why we act—or even feel— the way we do. The archetype at the core of the schizophrenia complex might manifest by our sense of losing track of who we are or feeling some threat of such an occurrence. Jung wrote:

> By ego I understand a complex of ideas which constitutes the centre of my field of consciousness and appears to possess a high degree of continuity and identity. Hence I also speak of *an ego-complex* . . . a psychic element [that] is . . . conscious to me only in so far as it is related to my ego-complex. But inasmuch as the ego is only the centre of my field of consciousness, it is not identical with the totality of my psyche, being only one complex among other complexes. . . . The ego is only the subject of my consciousness, while the self is the subject of my total psyche, which also includes the unconscious.[15]

For Jung, the individual ego complex not only exists relative to other complexes within the psyche, but also draws its stability and growth from a larger, archetypal wholeness. The ego has the job of adapting to both inner and outer existence. The maintenance of adequate ego stability has great bearing upon one's ability to keep the balance between consciousness and the unconscious, including a working relationship with the self. With schizophrenia, that balance is burst asunder. Unconscious contents impinge upon waking reality, threatening the stasis of conscious existence. Even the idea of such an experience, let alone an immediate encounter with it, understandably has the power to rattle our equilibrium.

At a seminar in my Jungian analytic training years ago, while I was only beginning to deal with my son's deep dive, training analyst Barry Williams made a comment that I found profoundly impactful in terms of my developing relationship with schizophrenia and our new family reality. His statement hints at the potential for something transformative in the "undoing" of one's life, at least as one has perceived it to be:

> The cure for psychopathology is to un-patholo-gize it. The 'just-so'-ness of life is the beauty of it, even if the ego is experiencing it as beautiful or unbearable. . . . There's no increase in conscious-ness without sacrifice. Sacrifice is part of individ-uation, and sacrifice is archetypal. . . . You have to go through the undoing of your life in order to have your life.[16]

I did feel "undone." My son's schizophrenia shook my life and the lives of those dearest to me to our foundations. I had not realized my core resistance to this fact or how deeply I had been affected, not only by what we had gone through but also by my own fundamental judgment about it. Barry's words struck home. Timely and piercing, they opened the possibility of a new telos of hope and meaning in a reality where I had been preoccupied with perceived loss and failure.

An individual caught in the maelstrom of madness may be unaware of their plight while psychotic, but once such a plight becomes conscious, even a glimpse of "ordinary reality" entails some degree of confrontation with the terror of experiencing extreme alienation. Most individuals with schizophrenia are not in a constant state of psychosis but emerge periodically— experiencing what a colleague calls "islands of clarity." Perhaps in those "clear" moments, such an individual is most susceptible to what I am referring to as the schizophrenia complex, as consciousness of the labyrinth in which one is lost means facing both the terrifying, raw otherness of one's own inner state and one's standing in the outer world. The resulting anguish is more neurotic than psychotic, a form of ego suffering—we are disturbed by how disturbed we are, rather than being completely lost in the dark without a compass.

These "islands of clarity" represent not only periods of cognitive coherence but a potential restoration of the affect that was lost during psychosis. When someone in a psychotic state begins to regain their ego, initially they may be able to remember details of the experience they have been through, but the associated affect may still be absent. When such an individual begins to recover their true feelings and emotions about that experience, they may be horrified, saddened, enraged, ashamed, or overwhelmed. In response, they are likely to retreat back into the oblivion of the netherworld, especially if they are not on medication.

My son told me that when he was on Venice Beach (in a psychotic state), he recalled a sense of "joy, freedom, independence like I hadn't felt before . . . open, strong, outgoing, adventurous with my mind." He also described,

> Being nuts, believing wholeheartedly in things
> that aren't real. I miss it in a way—and I don't.
> When I was not on meds I had more energy, but
> I couldn't live in society. The dream world is fun,
> but I enjoy having stability.

In hindsight about that period many years later, he reflected, "I was in pain the whole time I was in psychosis." He had restored that lost affect to his ego consciousness.

What is madness? Is it anything not like me? Is it anything in another person that rattles me, that threatens my own sense of ego mastery—of unshakable confidence and control? A most disturbing aspect of encountering the mood of a person in an altered state—be it anxious, scared, angry, or inconsolable, and be it the result of psychosis or other causes such as alcohol or drugs—is that our usual responses are inadequate or miss the mark altogether. A script is unfolding in which our part is suddenly written in another language. Sometimes being around a psychotic person can trigger compassion: we see their distress and want to comfort them, tell them not to be so sad, afraid, or foolhardy. Perhaps they scare us because they are clearly not connecting with us or the world around us as we perceive it to be. If we are close to the person, perhaps we are jolted because the one we knew so intimately stands before us in a familiar body they apparently no longer inhabit; in his or her stead is another entity, a stranger, leaving us feeling abandoned, craving the relationship we knew and loved.

Part of the schizophrenia complex is a vicarious—or projected—sense of distress. As we perceive the altered state of the other, we feel our own fear of isolation, alienation, abandonment—even annihilation. There are many ways to experience encounters with what we call schizophrenia, each of which is associated with an emotional state, often involving some form of inner disturbance.

Speaking of different kinds of disturbance, I remember a particular scene when my daughter and I went to visit my son on Venice Beach after he had been living there "homeless" for weeks. The whole environment was a macabre carnival: hot sunshine pouring everywhere, dogs, sand, drug dealers, street artists, kitschy beachfront shops, and ocean waves softly rumbling close by. The raucous thump of rap music bellowed incessantly from huge loudspeakers that blasted the same theme at routine intervals like cockamamie clockwork, a resounding background for the exaggerated gymnastics of street-performance artists.

My son had agreed to rendezvous with us at a given location in front of a tobacconist. He was barefoot, sunburned, and smiling. As we three strode the sunny beachside strip together at a rapid clip, he held my daughter gripped under one long arm and me under the other. He semi-lifted us off the ground as we traveled (he is six foot five), all of us laughing, my daughter and I in disbelief at the odd familiarity of stopping in a shop to buy him thongs and cigarettes as we might have done when he requested souvenirs on one of many family vacations in the past.

This scene, among others, was an experience of holding the tension of opposites. Meeting my son there, literally and figuratively, was poignant, beautiful—and heartbreaking. We entered his realm momentarily. He could scoop us up. We had a whiff of his reality as he experienced it. There was the joy and relief of reunion as well as the ache of knowing we were only visiting his delusional world; we could not really join him there and would not want to. At the same time, we so desperately did not want to leave him, to let him return to where we could not reach him again. We had a deeply felt sense of our rattled family love, against all odds. We were momentarily in sync, held together in a strong bond by Eros, the sweet god of relatedness, sharing a visceral connection that bridged the great abyss separating my son's perception of reality from our own.

My daughter and I later reflected on the weird feeling that we were being lifted along with him, each in his firm side hug. This was a sort of Mad Hatter's holiday, giddy and warped; but mostly I remember the sensation of literally being swept along with my son's delusions, probably more profoundly than we could realize or understand at the time. In that moment, our true affective responses of abject terror and sadness were somewhere off screen, perhaps deep in the unconscious. Of necessity, we were dropped into the immediacy of the moment—of *his* moment. I suppose in some regard we felt we were fighting for his life; later I would realize we were also trying to preserve our own lives—our sense of familiarity, normalcy, and reason. Only in hindsight can I begin to perceive with some objectivity the impact the experience of that time had upon our psychological and emotional survival—and subsequent development.

The Schizophrenia Complex and Trauma: Ambiguous Loss

Trauma often catalyzes a complex. As Jung stated, the trauma may be "either a single, definite violent impact, or a complex of ideas, emotions which may be likened to a psychic wound. . . . One could easily represent the trauma as a complex with a high *emotional charge* [emphasis added]."[17] One characteristic of schizophrenia is dissociated affect. The kind of emotional charge involved in a trauma complex would necessitate some conscious affect. Someone with schizophrenia may develop a complex in response to trauma, but only once they regain enough ego consolidation to connect with their lost affect and recover some ability to reflect upon their own experience. Others who encounter schizophrenia in a loved one may experience the onset of the condition and its ramifications as emotionally traumatic and end up with a schizophrenia complex as I am defining it—depending on how overwhelming and ego dystonic they find such an encounter.

I am using the term *schizophrenia complex* in a way akin to our typical understanding of a complex as feeling toned, accessible to some ego consciousness although relatively compartmentalized. Defined thus, the schizophrenia complex in a schizophrenic individual involves that individual's conscious feelings and emotions about his or her own psychotic condition. For example, when someone with schizophrenia starts to become aware of being looked at quizzically by others, and to feel (and express) the emotional impact of such observation, there is an opening of sorts. The affect consciously experienced by the individual is then accessible as a feeling-toned complex. The associated affect is no longer split off, fully autonomous and compartmentalized from consciousness. As such, to be able to be in a complex is a sign of recovery for someone with schizophrenia. To have a complex requires an ego that is not fully submerged in the unconscious. It requires a degree of consciousness, the ability to reflect and to name affects.

A schizophrenia complex as I am defining it is intrinsically different from early trauma-based complexes in which affect around a specific, overwhelming historical experience must be recovered. When someone with schizophrenia develops a complex, working through it in therapy or analysis entails the development of some objective capability—a particularly daunting challenge for an individual emerging from a world in which his or her only reality has been a subjective one. With a schizophrenic experience, affect associated with events may be completely dissociated until the individual develops the cognitive capability and ego stability to reclaim it. The ensuing complex is not anchored in early trauma; rather, the schizophrenia itself becomes the trauma once the ego begins to reconsolidate. One reason some individuals with schizophrenia have such difficulty and resistance to leaving the imaginal realm is that they lack sufficient ego consolidation to handle the trauma of recovering painful affect associated with their personal history of life changes that they did not choose. Even when they do gain the ego strength (typically with medication), reconciliation with the old life before the flood—before the ego became awash with archetypal contents—may be overwhelming to remember, at least initially.

General psychology uses the term *ambiguous loss* to refer to loss that lacks closure or understanding, whereby the impacted individual is left forever seeking answers, their grieving delayed and potentially unresolvable. The word *ambiguous* means "unclear," "uncertain," "obscure," and "indistinct." In relationships, an ambiguous loss of a loved one is characterized by a lack of facts to explain and assimilate what happened satisfactorily. What happens to family members dealing with schizophrenia in their midst is similar. What happens to individuals suffering schizophrenia themselves upon realizing the turn their lives have taken without their consent can also feel like an ambiguous loss. Ambiguous loss is disturbing to our egos, depressing and unsettling, just like dealing with schizophrenia can be. We have no clear category for the array of ways this odd phenomenon can manifest. We lack a clear way to predict, digest, control, treat, or respond to it.

With schizophrenia, the sense of loss is not traceable to a specific traumatic experience or wounding by an "other." Such a formless loss remains intangible but no less impactful than losses we can attribute to an identifiable, specific trauma. That ambiguity can be experienced as overwhelming. If such emotional content cannot be held consciously, a schizophrenia complex may result. The concept of ambiguous loss is one metaphorical image for the feeling of archetypal chaos that encountering schizophrenia can evoke. The trauma of encountering a familiar loved one who is physically present but psychologically absent and unfamiliar can lead to a state of utter confusion that can trigger defenses against such an intolerable emotional overload, resulting in an associated complex.

The Schizophrenia Complex:
Family Legacy

This book is inevitably about my own schizophrenia complex and also my family's. Jung knew that family complexes are handed down in a form of psychic inheritance. My son's illness has an ancestral component, according to what I have been able to discover—along with what, by my mother's choosing, I will never know. Whatever that legacy is in its entirety flows through me as well. Jung wrote, "Psychologically, the central point of a human personality is the place where the ancestors are reincarnated."[1] He also stated, "Nothing influences children more than the silent facts in the background."[2] The secret encapsulated trauma surrounding schizophrenia in my mother's family was an unspoken part of my psychic legacy that surfaced when I was forced to deal with the emergence of schizophrenia in my own. I choose to illuminate that history toward healing our family schizophrenia complex. Secrecy has not worked.

Certainly, anything about the reality of my maternal aunt's condition, and, even more so, how it radically affected my mother and her family of origin psychologically and emotionally was in the realm of "silent background" in my childhood. This remained so even after, as a young adult, I became persistent and direct in my efforts to unearth anything about this padlocked, generational family secret. Where did this hidden affect go—the fear, sadness, and shame—but into the shadow realm of the unconscious, a shared family shadow-field? There it would acquire well-defended archetypal proportions bearing a life of its own well beyond the obvious practical challenges of schizophrenia.

During my childhood, in my mother's audible silences, I sensed—intuited—that there was something hidden in her family, something wrong. Through a variety of experiences over decades, I became aware that what was wrong centered on the fact that her sister had been schizophrenic. From an early age, that shadow had impacted my mother and her family in ways I could never fully understand, simply because of the vast differences between us in culture, surroundings, and family circumstances. My mother grew up in a Swedish-American enclave with first- and second-generation Swedish parents in Cranston, Rhode Island. I grew up with my divorced, single mother in Berkeley, California, during its most radical period in the 1960s. Decades later, I became aware that when growing up, my mother had been repulsed and deeply embarrassed by her sister's illness. This reaction was certainly understandable, given everything else I dimly understand about their family dynamics, and the prevailing attitude of the times about any kind of mental illness. My mother had been forced to make do in her own headstrong way. She ultimately chose to say goodbye forever to her family home, her father, and her sister when she was still a young adult. She reinvented herself—even her name—after her sweet mother's untimely death at age fifty.

My mother referred to a "doom cloud" she had sensed since childhood. This image fit her personality: Although a bright woman, she had clearly suffered a trauma during her formative years that she was unable to outgrow and could not consciously heal. She spent her life with it haunting her periphery—a phenomenon I was aware of as a barely discernable but permanent backdrop of the obsessive–compulsive machinations she used to bind her anxiety about all that stuffed material. On various occasions throughout my life, my self–assigned role was to dispel her doom cloud by whatever means I could access. As a child, that meant doing things like drawing her pictures or writing her poems. When older, I would try to talk her through it from various perspectives reflecting my own stage of development, studies, and introspective process. At best, my lifelong efforts produced temporary fixes.

My mother's doom cloud might also be perceived as an image of a schizophrenia complex—a knot of relatively unconscious, unresolvable, unspeakable thoughts and emotions that had become symbolized for her by her schizophrenic sister. On an unconscious level, my mother's schizophrenia complex triggered my own, especially since I had no idea about this history until I was an adult. The family schizophrenia complex influenced the evolution of my psyche in ways I have only been able to examine with some objectivity since my mother's passing in 2014.

Particularly, as I wrestle with the reality of my son's illness, I have had to dig deep to find a broader perspective that liberates me from my own sense of doom. In that process, I had a realization that as terrifying as the disease can be, schizophrenia itself was not the essence of my mother's doom cloud; rather, it was the feeling-toned ramifications of it in her family, introjected deep in her psyche. That was the beginning of my thinking about a schizophrenia complex as something related to, but different from, schizophrenia itself.

My mother's family of origin was marred by the shadow of a horrific accident that occurred a generation before her birth. When my maternal grandfather was only a small child, all three of his older siblings drowned one afternoon while ice-skating—when the ice broke on a local pond. The emotional and psychological repercussions of this event at the time can only be imagined, although they will rustle through the generations of our family tree forever. The accident occurred in 1905 in a small Swedish community in Rhode Island. There was no therapy at the time, and most families were trying hard to appear as well adjusted and as "American" as possible.

During my mother's earliest years, the intolerable reality of the family's unspoken, inconsolable loss was naturally beyond my mother's understanding or ability to process—it was surely terrifying, inaccessible on any conscious level, and amplified to the astronomical proportions of a child's imagination. Moreover, all this implicit generational trauma became conflated with and represented by her sister's inexplicable, disturbing oddness. I think my mother's overwhelming experience of her sister's schizophrenia became symbolic of all that was wrong in an already dysfunctional family. In other words, my mother's sister became her repository for all that shadowy projected grief, shame, fear, and dread.

Schizophrenia became the symbolic container for all aspects of reality my mother could not accept. Avoiding facing those aspects of reality became tantamount to her survival and generalized into a strategy of avoiding all things peculiar or irrational—and the list grew from there. Ironically enough, this commitment to avoidance under the guise of a fundamentalist allegiance to logic shored up her iron-clad, magical thinking. Since this underpinning of her approach to reality was never discussed, despite my efforts, the magnitude of the "secret" remained frozen in time—petrified—throughout her life, imprisoned by her protective psyche, barred from her keen intellect. There was a part of my mother that was a willful, privately terrified child forever, determined to make a life anyway—which she certainly did, admirably so—with an energetic, steely determination that belied her tiny physical frame.

She was a powerhouse of sorts, a true Artemis, despite her doom cloud. In ancient Greek mythology, Artemis is the spirited goddess of the hunt and the moon, roaming the forests, the epitome of feminine independence. Part of my Artemis—mother's power over me was my awareness on some level that her doom cloud was hovering over me, too. But with her passing, and in an oddly synchronistic way, with the discovery of my son's condition, that cloud is gone for me. I realize that, although I have a profound respect for the intimidating nature of schizophrenia and would certainly opt to avoid or eradicate it if given the choice—my true reaction to the illness is less fear or shame than it is profound sadness.

Another part of my Artemis mother's power over me is a legacy to activate my own form of her iron perseverance. This legacy of perseverance takes the form of an unrelenting inner demand to consciously confront the charged phenomenon of what we call schizophrenia and its ramifications, within and beyond my family.

My son's struggle to hold onto ego consciousness influenced my own. The shock of his descent necessitated my conscious adjustment to these unforeseen, unwanted circumstances, as our family reality was rent asunder. In addition, on an unconscious level I felt I needed to hold onto an ego–Self axis, to stay connected to my core for my son when he could not.

41

Part of dealing with this challenge was differentiating between my inflated identification with the Great Mother archetype and my relationship with him as my Divine Child, and a realistic need to support him psychologically and emotionally through a period when I knew on every level that he lacked the ability to steer himself well. I am reminded of a dream snippet I had when he was a baby, which I now perceive as prospective. In the dream, I was swimming under water with him, tucked under one arm in a cross-chest lifeguard carry while I stroked with the other, propelling us forward together. I was calm and we were not drowning—we were conjoined in navigation.

Jung's famous diagram of the analytical relationship in *The Psychology of the Transference* shows the dynamic between consciousness and the unconscious in the analyst and analysand.[3] This idea can be applied in more general ways to describe the different levels upon which we relate to ourselves, each other, and life experiences. Because what we call schizophrenia fundamentally describes a relationship with the unconscious, its presence constellates our own shadow responses to unconscious contents. It is a reminder of something we cannot quite remember and probably would rather not—in addition to the conscious reactions we are aware of that may emanate from our own schizophrenia complexes, usually emotional responses of dread or avoidance. Personally and collectively, encounters with schizophrenic symptoms in others represent a form of confrontation with our own fears of unbearable affect and imagery.

In any complex, we say or do things unlike ourselves as we believe ourselves to be. Our own reactions may freeze us, numb us, or liberate an uncharacteristic lack of restraint: "I can't *believe* I said that!" In the throes of a schizophrenia complex, our behavior offers hints about its contents. When my son was in his, which only occurred as he began to recover some ego consolidation, he remembered a daring and ruthless independence he had not exhibited previously. When I was in mine, I sometimes found myself trying to join with him, to hold onto him to the point of an over-empathetic immersion, as if by psychic force I could keep him connected to me, to reality, to safety. Upon reflection, when my mother was in her schizophrenia complex, shortly before her death as she was faced with her beloved grandson's unexpected condition, she expressed outrage at him, accusing him of being manipulative. I think rage, repulsion, and rejection were her fierce defenses, an unconscious barricade against heartbreak.

When my son was deeply engulfed in his own unconscious, the person we knew and loved seemed unavailable; his ego was floating around in some eternal sea beyond our ken—and his own. On a conscious level, this was strange and worrisome for all kinds of logical reasons. On a deeper level of which we were only remotely aware at the time, our own innate fears of becoming unmoored were inevitably triggered. As for my son, when he first emerged from his deep dive months later, he, too, very slowly began the arduous process of beginning to experience from a conscious perspective his true emotional reactions to what he had been through and to have thoughts about what that meant for him in the arc of his life. That process has been ongoing for years. He now has a healthy respect for the journey he underwent and gratitude for a precious return never to be taken for granted. He did not end up playing professional basketball, the ubiquitous projection that enveloped him earlier in his life (which was never really his heart's desire, although he understandably lacked the ego strength to reject it). Nor did he end up sleeping on his cardboard square on the beach indefinitely. Neither of those persona identities seems to me to reflect his true self—if anything, they might be oddly related psychic bookends, the latter a sort of desperate, unconscious compensation for the former.

While my son's journey was solo in many ways, he did not undergo it alone. The schizophrenia complex is often a family affair. This upheaval in his life affected and transformed all of us profoundly. I image his life as a pebble thrown in a pond, the ripples circling ever wider. Broadening the lens reveals all our pebble lives, each plunk resulting in overlapping, ever-widening concentric circles: merging patterns in a shared body of water—a shared psychic life.

It was intolerable for my mother to perceive her only grandson—her beautiful, tall, intelligent, promising grandson—suffering from the blight she had spent a lifetime denying existed in her own family of origin. She passed away the year after my son metaphorically fell off the face of the earth, although he bounced back and forth between home and elsewhere during that time period. I have no doubt about the profound effect the emergence of her beloved grandson's illness had on her given her determination to avoid awareness of it in her sister—although outwardly she remained in adamant denial of his condition.

My own opposite reaction constellated a shift in the family field that has continued to unfold. I view these turns of events not as causal but synchronous; psyche granted us an opportunity disguised as loss. I did not shift my attitude with the goal in mind to heal the family tree. I never would have chosen this route. I was never able to make my mother feel any differently about schizophrenia, but I myself do. My natural response to the immediacy of my son's condition represented a shift in the psychic family legacy, although I identified it as such only afterward. I attribute that shift less to conscious effort than to Eros. All my previous, deliberate efforts to exorcise the family tree of its demons could occur only intellectually. Apparently, psyche—and life—demanded more.

My perception is that one aspect of my son's true self that emerged through his involuntary journey into the darkness of this illness is that he functions in the role of a scout. At the place where psyche meets ordinary reality, his travails—and our Eros-driven response to him—were necessary to change the relationship of our family to schizophrenia forever. In my mother's lifetime, dealing with schizophrenia evoked desperation associated with hidden terror, denial, shame, and radical severance. Ultimately, at this point in my life, we are in the uncharted territory of dealing with schizophrenia as a family, with an attitude of inclusion guided by love. Unwittingly, my son scouted new territory, and we followed. One never knows what shape the hero's journey will take, the greater good it will ultimately serve, or the hidden gold the transformational process of confrontation with our demons may yield.

Well before my son's experience with what we call schizophrenia, while I was growing up, there was the vague sense of something unstated and hovering that made its whisper-soft presence known to me as a slight, ever-present thrum of anxiety. I now identify that as a visit by the schizophrenia complex. This aspect of my life was functionally eclipsed, truly well-orchestrated by my mother, all things considered. I never meant to pass on such a legacy of silence: it came uninvited through me. I seriously doubt I could or would have faced it fully had I not been forced to do so. The possibility of genetic causality is less clear to me—and less important to me—than that of psychic inheritance, though I do not dismiss either. The challenge I resonate with is to confront this family complex of archetypal proportions that has been constellated through my son's experience. I view that turn of events not as mere coincidence, but as evidence of a potentially useful synchronicity, like a purposive dream. With this writing, my effort toward healing my ancestral schizophrenia complex joins my hope that doing so might also prove useful to others.

A Justifiable Terror

We humans are most comfortable with safe, brightly lit ego consciousness. The phenomenon of schizophrenia epitomizes the absolute polar opposite: chaos and darkness. We have deep layers of instinctual resistance to the mere idea of such a nebulous, potentially dangerous aspect to our existence. Yet the path to wholeness, to individuation, calls upon us to face that which we most want to avoid. To revisit Jung's quote of his soul speaking:

> Be silent and listen: have you recognized your madness and do you admit it? Have you noticed that all your foundations are completely mired in madness? . . . Do you not want to recognize your madness and welcome it in a friendly manner? You wanted to accept everything. So accept madness too. Let the light of your madness shine, and it will suddenly dawn on you. Madness is not to be despised and not to be feared, but instead you should give it life. . . . If you want to find paths, you should also not spurn madness, since it makes up such a great part of your nature. . . .

Be glad that you can recognize it, for you will thus avoid becoming its victim. Madness is a special form of the spirit and clings to all teachings and philosophies, but even more to daily life, since life itself is full of craziness and at bottom utterly illogical. Man strives toward reason only so that he can make rules for himself. Life itself has no rules. That is its mystery and its unknown law. What you call knowledge is an attempt to impose something comprehensible on life.[1]

Any encounter with schizophrenia carries an invitation to get in touch with our own madness. We would rather refuse, if given a choice. My sinkhole dream described in the preface presents just such a justifiable terror. The challenge of diving into that black, bottomless pool is not like walking a child to swim class and encouraging them to be unafraid, coaxing a step toward a positive development. Contrarily, it could represent a psychic dissolution that is not in service to individuation at all but a leap into nothing for nothing—at least not for a part of our existence we can know or own. Who in their right mind would choose that? In such an instance, wariness is healthy—maybe a healthy defense against being overwhelmed, against the threat of disintegration. The desire to avoid such an experience is reasonable—even self-preserving; it is to be afraid of the loss of our very sense of self. That dive into the bottomless, dark waters represents the annihilation of consciousness—of the ego, and the strength we work hard for, need, count on. We want to stay in that brightly lit room for understandable and legitimate reasons.

So, in the dream I recounted in the preface, why was I tempted—and even cajoled by myself (the dream ego, my inner gym teacher)—to dive into the pool and do my exercises, while every fiber of my being pulled away from the dreaded task? Perhaps because something in me, in us, does compel us to know more, to bring to consciousness what we can from the seeming black void of the unknown. That inner dialogue does seem in the service of individuation and may in fact be prerequisite. Here we have yet another tension of opposites: that safe, brightly lit room of ego consciousness juxtaposed with the boundless reaches of the dark unconscious. The nature of our human existence inevitably bridges both, and failure to balance the tension between these realities can be mortally destructive. The challenge of navigating these opposites is enough to strike justifiable terror into anyone's heart.

That challenge is archetypal. The stories of ancient Greece provide archetypal templates through which we can recognize and metaphorically access the myths we are living. The details change, but the same inner/outer conflicts play out in the world as they always have: chaos and order, the lure of madness and the need for balance. The tragic story of Pentheus, told by Euripides in *The Bacchae* in 405 BCE and later in Ovid's *Metamorphoses* in 8 CE, illustrates this conflict.[2]

Versions vary, but the overall theme is Pentheus's confrontation with the cult of Dionysus. Dionysus, also called Bacchus, was the nature god of fruitfulness, vegetation, wine, and ecstasy. When the latter two components went out of control, which they often did, dangerous havoc inevitably ensued. In *The Bacchae*, Pentheus was the grandson of the King of Thebes, who was in charge of keeping order. Dionysus was irresistibly popular at the time, devotedly followed by a female retinue, the *maenads*, whose name literally translates as "raving ones." When Dionysus and his maenads showed up in Thebes bringing unbridled, hedonistic revelry, Pentheus first tried unsuccessfully to banish him. He then tried to lock him up—also ineffective. Next, he tried to keep others from being in touch with the god, but Dionysius's pull was too strong, and he led his female followers into the wilderness out of the realm of Pentheus's authority. Eventually, Pentheus tracked Dionysus to a grove where the women of Thebes were dancing wildly. Pentheus was ostensibly there to arrest them, but he became too fascinated by the wild rites to carry out his mission. He hid in a nearby tree, a bewitched onlooker. The berserk women mistook him for an animal and attacked him as a sacrifice to consume, tearing him to pieces. In a gruesome twist, Pentheus's mother, Agave, one of the dancers, brought home his head, in her delirium not realizing what she had done.

As a myth, of course, this timeless story not only represents a truth about our dealings with each other in the world, but also symbolizes a dimension of our inner reality. If on a conscious level we are unprepared when we experience the inevitable attraction of the mad part of ourselves—the lure of the unconscious—we can figuratively be torn apart. It is significant that it is Agave who carries off his severed head. As Pentheus's mother, in her delirium she thus literally and symbolically truncates her own genetic legacy along with losing her mind. What a quintessentially alarming, visceral, gut-wrenching image of the annihilation that awaits us if we lose our balance, our ego consolidation, our overall bearings. Pentheus's mother is blindly caught up in the chaos of madness.

Symbolically, this scene could also be interpreted as a dream. Pentheus's beheading might suggest that Agave's own young, strong animus—her guiding, inner-masculine aspect—has been ruthlessly severed. Now she has no ruling, inner logos. The head, representing her vital capacity for logical, rational thinking, has been disconnected from the body, so she is driven by reckless instinct and unregulated affect. She is left with no mind or spirit functioning in any integrated way. Agave is frenzied—swept into the chaotic void of the unconscious without an anchor or a paddle—and look what it cost her!

We humans are inherently confronted with the dramatic opposites of order and chaos, and the challenge to regulate the interplay between ego development and the unconscious, in ways both personal and collective. One difference between the archetypal contents of the collective unconscious and other contents, such as those of the personal unconscious, is that sometimes walls are lifesaving. While "walls" may have a negative connotation, as though we are avoiding something that should be included or faced, boundaries and differentiation are generally acknowledged as positive functions, helping us to keep things—keep ourselves—together. Jungians tend to favor the idea of emulating Jung's own deep dive into the unconscious. Approaches to this diving process include efforts to humanize the intolerable archetypal aspects of the unconscious. Sometimes that is possible, at least partially. The story of Pentheus reminds us that caution is warranted.

Maybe the answer to my sinkhole dream is to continue honoring not knowing what to do, if anything. There was no one right response in that dream, but the confrontation with the choice to dive in was necessary. Now, I remain in that space of not knowing. That stance is important to me in depotentiating my own schizophrenia complex. This might be conceptualized in terms of the transcendent function: confrontation, standing in the liminal place of "between" versus "either-or"—and actively waiting. The unchosen turn-of-life events, my son's schizophrenia, has catapulted me into having to engage in an unexpected development of my own experience.

Our personal and collective relationship with schizophrenia poses an archetypal challenge. Responding to what we know as schizophrenia requires holding and navigating a tension of opposites: between order and chaos, the ego and the unconscious. Even conscious recognition of that quandary may manifest as a voracious schizophrenia complex, a knot of unresolvable thoughts and emotions that represent a failure to hold the tension. For example, as I have mentioned, siblings of people with the condition often describe extreme anxiety and fear about whether they, too, are "going crazy"—and as a result may become hypervigilant and insecure about their own reality testing. A former psychological assistant of mine, whose brother had schizophrenia, described the following scene that occurred soon after the jarring onset of his symptoms: She entered her dark apartment at the end of a work day to hear the murmur of muffled voices. For a brief, agonizing moment she was sure it was her own auditory hallucination rather than the radio she had left on that morning.

Such a complex can occur both in those closest to an individual suffering schizophrenic symptoms and in collective entities and institutions. It can also occur in the symptomatic individual themselves, when the mist clears and reentry looms. It can occur anywhere—on the street corner, in the park, or in the grocery line. The world is a stage, and these afflicted players are often strikingly noticeable due to their bizarre behavior. In general, no one wants to be so "othered" or to be close to one so "othered." Furthermore, if one *is* connected to another so afflicted, that connection can potentially invoke judgment, fear, and rejection by others—rendering that affiliation a source of emotional angst. Such a relationship can be fraught with conflict between deep love and terror, heart-wrenching compassion and the desire for avoidance.

Jung had an extremely rare ability to navigate these murky waters and keep his ship afloat. During the period of his life when he was experiencing vivid encounters with his unconscious, both personal and collective—while reeling from his break with Freud and creating the material we now know as *The Red Book*—he consciously engaged the content that was erupting in him, and gave it creative outlet. This included spending dedicated time daily on the shore of Lake Zurich collecting, as he put it, "suitable stones" and constructing "cottages, a castle, a whole village." He adds, "I went on with my building game after the noon meal every day, whenever the weather permitted. As soon as I was through eating, I began playing, and continued to do so *until the patients arrived* [italics mine]."[3] This "schedule" clearly demonstrates deliberately holding the tension of the opposites—conscious and unconscious, inner and outer.

In a recent publication, British author Nathan Filer, a mental-health nurse, alludes to the incredible impact of schizophrenia—even the *word*—not only upon the immediate sufferer but upon the rest of us. He is hopeful that it is possible to have a shift in consciousness around schizophrenia while honoring the archetypal scope of this problem, emphasizing its emotional impact. He writes the following about schizophrenia:

> What a word, huh? I wonder if you might consider trying something for me? Say the word "schizophrenia" out loud a few times. Not beneath your breath. Really say it. Say it loud enough that you feel self-conscious; that you worry someone

will hear. Say it loud enough that someone might hear. Feel the shape of it. Stay with it. Think about what that word evokes in you. What thoughts does it arrive with? What feelings? . . . Please remember this as you do so: whole lives have disappeared beneath that word.[4]

Although described as a thought disorder, the lived experience of schizophrenia is mired in the realm of affect—both for those afflicted whose own conscious feeling associations are lost and for those others affected by their loved one's heartbreaking unavailability. Schizophrenia attacks relatedness through a confluence of factors, including emotional disconnection and the feelings of otherness, shame, and stigma that surround this experience—for everyone it touches.

This from my son, in a fairly recent reflection:

When I was psychotic, I was angry at anyone who came in my way. So, my feelings toward you were ultimately defiant. I look back in retrospect and realize that it was about having freedom to do what I wanted to do and I didn't have a liking for rules and discipline. Once I regained some reality to my life, I was calmer and more patient, which in turn gave me the ability to love and care for you and the ones I love. As time went on and I continued to take medication, I began to feel the connection we once had. I would say that respect is the one aspect that is most prevalent with me toward you and the whole family. When I was psychotic, I really didn't think about anybody but myself; that has completely changed as well. I look forward to helping others and you, and also myself. . . . There is positive communication that is caring and understanding, along with being able to sympathize.

My son was living an archetypal life. His car was his chariot, and when it was gone (we found it and took it, in a failed attempt to get him home), it did not matter; he wandered. He soared with the angels, and when he landed he was severely sunburned: echoes of Icarus. The physical injuries he had sustained suddenly came to his conscious attention. Reentry was slow and painful. To quote him from the arrival side of the gaping brink of his journey:

First, and most importantly, I had the love and support of my family. I don't know what I would be doing without the love and support of you guys. I put myself in many situations that made me stuck on an island, and you gave me a lifeboat to living.

What reels us back to land from the far reaches of the unconscious? There is no one answer. Perhaps we have to come apart in order to reconstitute the lives we were meant to have, sacrificing the script written by ego (as I was challenged to do)—or salvaging an ego flooded by the unconscious (as my son was challenged to do). Sometimes it is love that reels us back; inevitably, sometimes it is the opposite. In *Two Essays on Analytical Psychology*, Jung included the following from Freud's posthumous writings about two basic instincts, Eros and Death:

The aim of [Eros] is to establish ever greater unities and to preserve them thus—in short, to bind together; the aim of [the destructive instinct] is, on the contrary, to undo connections and so to destroy things. . . . For this reason, we also call it the *death instinct*.[5]

Jung comments,

Life, like any other process, has a beginning and an end and . . . every beginning is also the beginning of the end. What Freud probably means is the essential fact that every process is a phenomenon of energy, and that all energy can proceed only from the tension of opposites.[6]

The complicated interplay of energies that resulted in the return of my son to solid ground undoubtedly included both destruction and love; both were necessary. There was the destruction of the old order of our lives, inner and outer, and the power of love that allowed us to remain connected throughout that arduous journey. My prevailing image was of stubbornly digging a channel through bedrock driven by my yearning for relatedness, so that love—Eros—could find a way.

Jung's History with Schizophrenia

Schizophrenia deeply affected Jung's professional and personal life and seeded the development of his seminal theories. Jung's discovery of the collective unconscious and the function of archetypes ultimately arose from his own dreams and visions, but it was galvanized by his early, serious investigation of the fantasies of his schizophrenic patients. His empirical interpretations of those visions provide an excellent example of an autonomous manifestation of the unconscious.

As a young doctor, Jung did his psychiatric residency while living on the second floor of the Burghölzli, the psychiatric hospital in Zurich, under the mentorship of the hospital's director, Eugen Bleuler. That immersive work essentially taught Jung about the mythopoetic nature of the unconscious. One defining difference between Freud and Jung was Jung's work with psychotic patients, which opened him to the mystery, chaos, and formlessness of the unconscious. As such, Jung's immersion in this material with his patients at the Burghölzli was invaluable. This venture also demonstrated Jung's unique courage in terms of being willing to delve into that formidable milieu, inner and outer, with curiosity and openness. Certainly, this capacity served him during his own encounters with the unconscious, documented most notably in *The Red Book*.

Eugen Bleuler and Emil Kraepelin were preeminent medical doctors in the early twentieth century when the profession of psychiatry was initially developing. They established treatment protocols and developed theories that provided a medical model of schizophrenia. They strongly influenced Jung's understanding of patients with psychotic illnesses. With Bleuler, Jung used scientific research and a new conceptualization of human psychology to create what was then an entirely new disease concept: the schizophrenias. Jung's seminal complex theory emerged from his work with the word association experiments during this period.[1] He and his colleague Franz Riklin Sr. performed these experiments on patients who were both normal and psychotic within the psychiatric hospital. Jung eventually proposed that complexes are seen in *all* human beings, both those who are "normal" and those with schizophrenia.[2]

Jung's famous word association experiments during this time changed psychiatry forever. By measuring patients' physiological responses via their reaction times to a list of chosen words and then analyzing the results, he demonstrated the reality and autonomy of unconscious complexes. This realization not only proved that unconscious factors are at work within us, it led him to discover the universal human substrate of the collective unconscious: the deeper waters inherent to humankind.

It was Eugen Bleuler who figured out the value of applying the study of association patterns (including measures of attention and feeling tone) to psychotic patients in order to examine the inner workings of their condition scientifically. This approach in and of itself represented a significant departure from Kraepelin's diagnosis of schizophrenia as dementia praecox, a form of early dementia—because Bleuler's hypothesis opened the possibility that these patients' hallucinations and delusions had meaning and were not simply byproducts of neurological degeneration. Jung took this discovery much further as he continued his studies, ultimately bridging the hallucinations of some of his patients with archetypal themes. His work at the Burghölzli was instrumental in his conceptualization of the collective unconscious, one of the foundational concepts of his work.

A prototypical example of this development in his thinking arose through his work with a schizophrenic patient, known as the "solar phallus man." In 1906, one of his patients at the hospital had been diagnosed as an incurable paranoid schizophrenic. This man was uneducated and at times very disturbed, but during quiet periods he was able to communicate his visions and ideas to the doctors. One day, Jung discovered him standing by the window, moving his head from one side to the other and blinking into the sun. The patient brought Jung to the window and entreated him to do the same, as then he would see something interesting.

Jung asked what the man was seeing and the man responded, "Surely, Doctor, you will see the tail of the sun, the sun's penis. When I move my head to and fro, it moves, too, and that is where the wind comes from."[3]

At the time, Jung knew nothing of mythology or archaeology. The encounter puzzled him, but he made note of it.

About four years later—in 1910, when Jung was engrossed in mythological studies—he discovered the well-known philologist Albrecht Dietrich's *A Mithras Liturgy*, in which he recognized the delusional material of his former patient. This book from a famous Paris library published a Greek papyrus dealing with a Mithraic ritual for the first time. The relevant passage as Jung excerpted it reads as follows:

> Draw breath from the rays, draw in three times as strongly as you can . . . and you will seem to be in the middle of the aerial region . . . the path of the visible gods will appear through the disk of the sun who is God, my father. Likewise, there will be seen the so-called tube, the origin of the ministering wind. For you will see hanging down from the disk of the sun, something that looks like a tube. And towards the region westward, it is as though there were an infinite east wind. But if the other wind should prevail towards the regions of the east, in like fashion you will see the vision veering in that direction.[4]

The striking similarity between the hallucination of his patient and the Mithraic liturgy prompted Jung to investigate further, leading to his discovery of many parallels between motifs in the mythologies of various ethnic groups, and the visions and dreams of people who had never heard of them. This led him to conclude that there are myth-forming structural elements in the unconscious.[5] This realization was instrumental to his understanding of the collective unconscious and the archetypes. It also suggests that this kind of autonomous expression of the psyche is involved in producing the hallucinations and delusions of schizophrenia.

Jung's discovery that this man's psychotic fantasy was in fact a myth was monumental! This raised it to a meaningful story instead of just a madman's delusion to be dismissed, ignored, feared, or medicated away. This discovery and Jung's attitude about it, in a sense, humanized psychosis. At least ideologically, such a discovery had the potential to impact prevailing emotional responses to schizophrenia: the terrain of the schizophrenia complex. Jung's observation suggested that while we may perceive people with schizophrenia as different in kind, they are but different in degree. He later profoundly expressed his unique capacity to relate to his own irrational interiority in *The Red Book*. Universally, we human beings are mythmaking creatures.

In 1906, Jung wrote two articles on the word association test showing how it could be utilized to identify complexes that contribute to psychiatric illness.[6] In 1909, he developed his ideas further in his next major work, *The Psychology of Dementia Praecox*. He first posited the idea of relating complexes to psychiatric symptoms with regard to hysteria. That particular diagnosis was prevalent at the time, but the idea is relevant to schizophrenia—and for our purposes, the schizophrenia complex—as well. Jung wrote, "The complex has an abnormal autonomy in hysteria and a tendency to an active separate existence, which reduces and replaces the constellating power of the ego-complex."[7] The issue of a poorly functioning ego, which he recognized as one of many complexes (although clearly a centrally important one), remained instrumental to the subsequent work he and Bleuler did trying to understand and treat schizophrenia.

In other words, Jung determined that effective treatment for schizophrenia needed to incorporate, even emphasize, a restoration and strengthening of the ego. A strong or well-developed ego complex is needed to bracket and organize the unconscious contents that are constellated in schizophrenia. This idea is a central theoretical contribution to our understanding of this mysterious phenomenon.

Many other prolific Jungian writers and thinkers have enriched our understanding of this mysterious illness with creativity and insight beyond the realm of physical medicine: R. D. Laing, an anti-psychiatry psychiatrist, and J. W. Perry, a Zurich-trained Jungian analyst and psychiatrist, were two such pioneers (see further discussion in ch. 6). I find the available theoretical, philosophical, and even scientific knowledge about schizophrenia inarguably helpful, but ultimately less than satisfying or conclusive in terms of practical application toward prevention, treatment, or cure.

Having been blindsided by wholly unanticipated personal encounters with what we call schizophrenia so close to home has required me to adopt a new perspective on the family history my mother took pains to hide, and broaden it from there. Now I am struck by the need to conceive of this illness in terms that integrate the personal, collective, and archetypal—both for those suffering with schizophrenia, those affected by them, and those attempting to treat the illness.

Theories about Schizophrenia

What it is actually like for those suffering from schizophrenia and those closest to them—the maelstrom of feelings and emotions generated by the condition—is my focus in writing on the schizophrenia complex. Far less research has been done about the experience of an encounter with schizophrenia than about schizophrenia itself, about which there are many theories. In Jung's era, Emil Kraepelin first described schizophrenia in 1896, and Swiss psychiatrist Eugen Bleuler first used the term *schizophrenia* in 1911. Since then, a plethora of theories have continued to emerge about what schizophrenia is and what causes it, with implications for management and treatment.

This chapter can give but a rudimentary sense of the broad spectrum of academic research about this mysterious phenomenon. In it, I focus on those concepts that throughout the history of psychology have informed and reflected our emotional responses to the disorder, along with our thinking. Our various clinical approaches to working with psychosis are inevitably influenced by our feelings and emotional responses to the phenomenon along with our intellectual ideas—and vice versa.

Findings from Jung's word association experiment, became fundamental to diagnosing dementia praecox as well as to renaming the disease *schizophrenia*. The renaming is significant, representing a theoretical paradigm shift. Kraepelin's term, *dementia praecox*, literally translates to mean "early dementia." He believed the condition to be mainly a brain disease, a form of dementia. Bleuler's term, *schizophrenia*, is from the Greek *schizo*, "split," and *phrene*, "mind." He identified positive and negative symptoms and emphasized affective and psychological factors contributing to a splitting of *psychic*—as opposed to *neurological*—functioning. (For the past several decades, there have been various international movements to change the terminology of the schizophrenic condition. Since 1993, for instance, a movement has been afoot in Japan to replace the name *schizophrenia* with *integration disorder*, among other alternatives, essentially in hopes of reducing the stigma associated with the label.[1]

Ego psychology is a school of psychoanalysis rooted in Freud's structural id-ego-superego model of the mind. That theoretical perspective perceives such a framework as underlying an individual's interactions with the external world as well as their responses to internal forces. Historically, adherents of ego psychology focused on the ego's normal and pathological development, its management of libidinal and aggressive impulses, and its adaptation to reality.[2] For decades, the ideas of ego psychologists held sway in the fields of medical science and psychiatry. Unfortunately, though, while those ideas were academically sound and sophisticated, their implications regarding the causality of schizophrenia had devastating results for schizophrenic children and their families. These theorists posited that if the *physical* care of an infant was survivable but *emotionally* he or she were deserted or pushed beyond coping capacity, the infant would become autistic or schizophrenic, or die.[3] Attributing psychosis to parental failure is consistent with the theoretical perspective that the genesis of schizophrenia is an emotional and psychological defense response.

Not surprisingly, this attitude ultimately evoked guilt and shame for affected families. Parents—especially mothers—and their lack of adequate parenting were blamed for the disorder; they were considered guilty of causing it, and the identified patient was perceived as damaged goods as a result. The family carried the shame of both the "inadequate" parenting and the ill child. That emotional climate was fertile ground for the development of schizophrenia complexes, as the entire subject was understandably nearly intolerable for those impacted by it.

Hence, from the late 1940s to the early 1970s, schizophrenia was widely believed by psychologists to be a deliberate defense mechanism, a psychotic reaction to years of malicious and undermining parenting by the so-called "Refrigerator Mother." This was an essentially ego-psychology viewpoint, theorizing that schizophrenia developed when a child did not successfully connect with the mother. During that time, the concept of the "schizophrenogenic mother" as the cause of schizophrenia was popular in the psychiatric literature.[4]

From the perspective of my own experience with my son, certainly with the onset of his symptoms, I racked my brain trying to decipher all I had or had not done to warrant this extremely unwelcome turn of events. In regard to the Refrigerator Mother idea, I was never unavailable or emotionally disconnected from my children. I felt no shame about my son's condition, only fear and worry about his safety and deep sadness about the shattering of my preconceived picture of his future and, by extension, our family's. As a parent, guilt comes naturally and easily for me, but I also realize that guilt and shame lead nowhere but to more of the same—eventually resulting in a kind of soul-stymying self-pity that helps no one. Taking responsibility is another matter. Jung encouraged us neither to deny nor try to redeem our sins but instead to carry them.[5] Part of dealing with my own schizophrenia complex has involved holding enough tolerance for my perceived culpability for my son's condition to remain curious about it. As kitchen appliance analogies go, I was no refrigerator but more of an oven.

The ego-psychology idea that Refrigerator Mothers are essentially to blame may be a destructive patriarchal misreading rather than a complete inaccuracy, falling short but containing an important truth. The relationship with parents is inarguably influential. In my case, for example, the "oven" may have been too hot: upon reflection, perhaps I was too intense a parent to my son for reasons of my own, invested and involved in his inner and outer life in ways he experienced as psychological pressure.

This insight is most useful not as a one-sided shaming or blaming but as a field phenomenon of the psychological relationship between the child and the parents—perhaps particularly the mother—and the development of what we call schizophrenia. There appears to be a link, but not a linear one—not a clear causality.

Jung comprehended schizophrenia from a psychological point of view as well as an organic one; he embraced the importance of both factors and their interaction. Jung defined a schizophrenic condition as a personality split, a dissociation severe enough that it "reaches the organic structure."[6] As he put it in *The Psychogenesis of Mental Disease*,

I incline to the view that, on the basis of a disposition whose nature is at present unknown to us, an unadapted psychological function arises which may develop into a manifest mental disturbance and *secondarily* induce symptoms of organic degeneration.[7]

Scottish psychiatrist Ronald David Laing (1927–1989), usually cited as R. D. Laing, and Jungian analyst/psychiatrist John Weir Perry (1914–1998) studied and wrote extensively on the experience of psychosis. Their perspectives presented a stark contrast to the normative medical model of the definition, meaning, and best treatment of schizophrenia.

Laing's views on the causes and treatment of psychopathological phenomena were influenced by his study of existential philosophy and ran absolutely counter to the chemical and electroshock methods that had become standard practice. He argued that insanity could be a creative and adaptive response to the world and developed the theory that mental illness was actually an escape mechanism that allowed individuals to free themselves from intolerable circumstances—primarily emotional and psychological. What one experiences as intolerable emotionally and psychologically is a subjective reality not always evident from the outside. By way of illustration, at the point of my son's departure, despite his seemingly more-than-tolerable lifestyle, he still experienced an intolerable state of unrest. His leaving for Venice Beach was a literal and symbolic gesture of this truth—his subjective, inarguable truth, regardless of how anyone from the outside may have perceived his circumstances.

Perceiving the expressed feelings of the individual patient as valid descriptions of their lived experience rather than as symptoms of mental illness, Laing regarded "schizophrenia" as a theory rather than a fact. He was considered a rebel in the field of psychiatry. Perhaps he brought a fitting—even necessary—polar opposite attitude to the prevailing, condemning cultural response to mental illness. He wrote:

> If the human race survives, future men will, I suspect, look back on our enlightened epoch as a veritable Age of Darkness. . . . They will see that what was considered "schizophrenic" was one of the forms in which, often through quite ordinary people, the light began to break into our all-too-closed minds.[8]

Perry authored many books, including *The Self in Psychotic Process*, *The Heart of History*, and *Trials of the Visionary Mind*. Known as a radical thinker in the mental-health field, Perry believed that schizophrenia had benefits, and that the psychotic state could lead to higher consciousness if allowed to run its course. He described how stress may cause highly activated mythic images to erupt from the psyche's deepest levels in the form of turbulent visionary experience. Depending on whether the interactions between the individual and their immediate surroundings lean toward affirmation or invalidation, comprehension of these visions can turn the visionary experience either into a step toward growth *or* into a psychotic disorder.

Based on his clinical and scholarly investigations, Perry conceptualized a mental syndrome that, though customarily regarded as acute psychosis, is actually a natural effort of the psyche to mend its imbalances. Consequently, according to Perry, if the upset is received in the spirit of empathy and understanding and allowed to run its course, an acute episode can be found to reveal a self-organizing process that has healing potential. Jungians might call this an example of the self-regulation of the psyche, a function in waking life that is analogous to dreams. Perry noted the function of mythic themes, rituals of antiquity, and the visionary experiences undergone by prophets and social reformers in various ages and parts of the world as representative of this mysterious phenomenon and relevant to understanding it.[9]

Because of its roots in the scientific method, the medical model can only really incorporate phenomena that are measurable and quantifiable. This approach accords well with the physical or organic components of illness, but offers much less assurance with other factors, the most important of which are psychological and perhaps spiritual: whole person, whole family, external stressors, and inner emotional conflicts. Each person who has schizophrenia also has a plethora of *other* personality characteristics that do not disappear with the onset of psychosis and that matter tremendously. Each manifestation of schizophrenia is as unique as the individual who bears its symptoms—and the label. Those other personality characteristics affect how and whether the symptoms of schizophrenia are coped with and the degree to which they define a person and their functioning in the world. These characteristics include, but are certainly not limited, to introversion/extraversion, strength or weakness, tenacity or passivity, eros or destructive anger, capacity and initiative for relatedness, anxiety, depression, obsessiveness, organizational abilities, and level of intelligence. These qualities are not as binary as this list may sound but present along a continuum. All these personal character qualities combine with an individual's psychotic symptoms in an interactive, unique synergy. This is one reason why there is no consensually established, universally applicable diagnostic checklist of causes or symptoms or treatment protocols for all that we call schizophrenia.

External factors are another extremely powerful set of influences on how schizophrenia impacts an individual's potential level of functioning. These factors include home environment, family attitude, presence or absence of positive supports, work or school, and treatment and medication, to name a few. It comes down to what kind of container is available to the affected person. Absent a reliable internal locus of control, external supports can be crucial. Yet treatments and resources that really grapple with individual, nuanced manifestations of schizophrenia are extremely rare.

The archetypal dimensions of the meaning of schizophrenia are inevitably and inextricably interwoven with the more pragmatic and tangible. Both are important. Interacting with schizophrenia is in some ways like interacting with dreams— although emerging from an episode is less predictable than awakening from a dream. Just as Jung's work with the solar phallus man demonstrated, given the capacities for insight, reflection, interpretation, and association, mythopoetic meaning can be identified in the ego-dissociated visions of schizophrenia and can thus emerge into consciousness, given language. Without those capacities, however, the cord between consciousness and the unconscious dangles, and meaning may seem absent even though it is there, untapped, like a disconnected telephone line from the unconscious.

Chronic mental illness certainly is a brain disease, but that explains little, since *everything* is the brain—not just psychosis but our deeply irrational love for our spouses and children, for example. To end our understanding and inquiry about schizophrenia by defining it as a "brain disease" diminishes the other vital dimensions of what makes us human: our perceptions, our emotional intelligence, our souls. That reductive attitude posits that essentially nothing is real unless we can measure it. Mind, meaning, and experience are housed in the brain. Hippocrates wrote about this idea many centuries ago: "From nothing else but thence come joys, delights, laughter, and sports, and sorrows, griefs, despondency, and lamentations. And by the same organ we become mad and delirious, and fears and terrors assail us."[10]

The scientific worldview we have held is limited. The questions raised by twentieth-century quantum physicists introduced a perspective much broader than that of the old, mechanistic, materialistic, reductive model of the universe. Plenty was left out of that earlier worldview. Classical physics, developed largely by Isaac Newton (1643–1747), engaged in the study of physical objects observable at the *macrocosmic* level that behave with clockwork predictability: the apple always falls from the tree. Quantum physics, in contrast, focuses on the hidden, *microcosmic* level where particles and waves, matter and energy, paradoxically behave like one another, producing random outcomes. The Newtonian, rigid cause-and-effect model of classical physics is superseded, and predictions can be made based only on probability.

We can draw an analogy here between the classical conception of the brain as a strictly physical organ and the more contemporary speculations about the mystery of consciousness. In the early nineteenth century, the scientific worldview undergirding the Industrial Revolution that saw everything in terms of mathematically measurable elements prompted the rise of the Romantic poets such as Coleridge, who complained that post-Newtonian science had made of the earth a "lifeless machine."[11] His lament can be seen to foreshadow what is currently still a struggle—to conceptualize consciousness as more than a brain function. Philosophically, the existence and importance of the brain as a physical, scientific entity is inarguable—but so is the existence and importance of the mind. The brain is an organ, but the mind is not. The brain is the physical space where the mind resides. The mind manifests thought processes, perception, emotion, reason, and imagination. Newton and the other scientists gave us one kind of sense, Coleridge and Blake and the other philosophical Romantic poets another. This same duality manifests in our understanding of schizophrenia and our attitudes about it, as individuals and in society.

It stands to reason that, given the collective climate of extreme polarization in the world today, schools of thought in the diverse field of psychology are divided in their theoretical and treatment approaches to schizophrenia—in some ways mirroring the longstanding differences between medical psychiatry, ego psychology, and philosophical freelancers such as Laing and Perry. One unfortunate ramification of these differences is that resources for those suffering from schizophrenia and their families and communities are inconsistent, if not absent.

The dearth of resources and lack of responsiveness to this problem might also be more than a bureaucratic failure; it might represent a collective schizophrenia complex at the institutional level, showing up as social policy that is stingy and ill conceived. The disavowal of responsibility can be construed as an indirect—perhaps even unconscious—expression of rejection and avoidance. Beneath the failure to provide accessible, effective resources for those dealing with schizophrenia may lie an archetypal bedrock of fear of the other, the not-me, expressed thorough a lack of support and viable options provided collectively. Better understanding of and more effective management and response to this essentially archetypal illness requires a spirit of curiosity and inclusion. At the very least, on a conscious level, this problem suggests the need for clinicians to have an open dialogue, to discuss and question our beliefs about schizophrenia and advocate for resources. Doing so might also represent the depotentiation of a collective schizophrenia complex through conscious action.

Jung came along eons before neurotechnology enabled scientists to peer inside the human brain and identify the physiological manifestations of schizophrenia. More recent scientific discoveries enhance our understanding and ability to treat the disease, but these newer developments fall short of illuminating the broader archetypal nuances of this phenomenon, which Jung helped us decipher. Blind (or even informed) devotion to exclusively scientific explanations for phenomena that transcend them is an understandable defense. There are emotional reasons we get doggedly attached to our defenses and our theories—they bind anxiety and fear.

Psychiatric science has continued to discover more about possible origins of schizophrenia as well as contributing and compensatory factors and new treatment strategies, including improved antipsychotic medications. The dopamine hypothesis of schizophrenia was formulated in the 1960s: that the unusual behavior and experiences associated with schizophrenia—sometimes extended to include psychosis in general—can be fully or largely explained by changes in dopamine function in the brain. Not coincidentally, this hypothesis corresponded with the arrival of a touted new wonder drug to treat it, after the discovery of the antipsychotic actions of chlorpromazine. Chlorpromazine is now known by its well-known brand name, Thorazine. Thorazine has a list of draconian side effects, as the vast majority of psychotropic medications still do. At the negative extreme, its side effects include Parkinsonian symptoms and sudden death. It continues to be used to treat schizophrenia, although less often than when it was first introduced.

In 2016, scientists broke new ground in the study of schizophrenia by uncovering a potentially powerful genetic contributor to the mental disorder that helps to explain why its symptoms of confused and delusional thinking most often coincide with young adulthood. In short, immune-related genetic variations linked to schizophrenia play a key role in prompting the natural pruning of brain synapses in normal, late-adolescent development. In individuals with schizophrenia, excessive pruning occurs, leading to the thought disorder.[12] Exactly what to do with that information remains vague. Current research supports the idea that excessive brain pruning is a factor in the development of schizophrenia, but not as an exclusive explanation or definitive cause and without prescriptive ramifications at this point.

Overall, research (and common sense) suggest that a combination of physical, genetic, psychological, and environmental factors can make a person more or less likely to develop what we call schizophrenia. Some people may be prone to the condition but maintain marginally balanced functioning until a stressful or emotional life event triggers a psychotic episode. For some who are prone, it takes almost nothing externally to trigger them into a psychosis. Others may be prone, but coexisting personality characteristics— tenacity and a strong ego, for example—may overrule the propensity. In still others not "prone" per se, a trauma unsettling enough to flood a typically stable ego may produce a psychotic experience. The developmental crisis of entering and adjusting to adulthood may fall into the latter category for some individuals.

The exact causes of schizophrenia remain unknown; the definition remains unclear; and ideas about medication and treatment remain inadequate, potentially damaging, and, most of all, inconsistent. Each of the theoretical perspectives and findings mentioned above has something to offer and warrants consideration, but none of them provide definitive answers on the causes, the most effective treatment approach, or the possibility of prevention.

Psychological, emotional, developmental, biological, and even metaphysical influences seem to be at play in this phenomenon, but not in the same way in each individual who develops schizophrenic symptoms. There are endless possibilities of combinations of contributing factors that create a unique synergy in each individual case that determine whether and how a psychosis emerges. Jung's approach was at least descriptive rather than dogmatic. By bridging the unconscious chaos inherent in the condition to the potential mythopoetic meaning therein, he overrides fear with curiosity and leaves room for whatever we cannot predict or know. That expansive attitude holds healing potential for the schizophrenia complex triggered by dread of this mysterious condition.

The hardest reality about schizophrenia is that we *do not know* definitively what it is, what causes it, or how to make it go away. However, that reality does not stop us from generating theories—to the contrary. With all due respect for science and existential philosophy, there seems to be a desperation about our fervor to understand, explain, and find an answer to this condition. We are unceasing in our efforts to reel in this vaporous creature that ostensibly steals lives on the cusp of adulthood. Our efforts are understandable because schizophrenia can be terrifying and destructive. We are compelled to make sense of it, although the immutable bottom line is the one we collectively avoid most stringently: it is a mystery.

A common denominator in all theorizing about schizophrenia is our deep human need to solve essentially insoluble mysteries, or at least agree about a meaning. When such efforts fail, unwanted emotions can be triggered and a complex likely ensues. Part of the repulsion and avoidance that surrounds schizophrenia is the archetypal frustration constellated by our inability fully to understand or to solve it. An encounter with schizophrenia reminds us of our ultimate humility before the unconscious, that great sea that rumbles always beneath our neat lives.

It seems we cannot stop trying to bring this most chaotic manifestation of the unconscious under conscious control. These efforts to tame—or slay—the monster, while heroic, also point out (as Jung did) the pitfalls of the heroic stance. Like a riddle in a fairytale, schizophrenia demands submission and tolerance when such an attitude is absolutely ego-dystonic; it demands that in some way we accept and befriend it instead of trying to master it. This seems an extreme example of Jung's idea that *"the experience of the self is always a defeat for the ego."*[13] My egoic defeat by schizophrenia is like a dive into the deep pool in the dream I described in the preface. At first the experience was a shock to my system; then, to preserve life, I discovered a new way to breathe. Even still, momentarily, I forget how. In those moments, I am revisited by my schizophrenia complex.

Alchemical Implications: The Solutio

The following discussion of the alchemical implications of schizophrenia focuses on the mystery of the phenomenon itself. The relevance of this emphasis to the schizophrenia complex is that our further understanding of schizophrenia may help illuminate its intense emotional ramifications; what we are unable to tolerate consciously goes into a complex. The alchemical dimensions of schizophrenia help to explain the potentially overwhelming archetypal scope of its meaning for us psychologically and emotionally.

Jung's understanding of alchemical symbolism was fundamental to his ideas about unconscious processes, including schizophrenia. In his autobiography, he wrote:

> Only after I had familiarized myself with alchemy did I realize that the unconscious is a *process*, and that the psyche is transformed or developed by the relationship of the ego to the contents of the unconscious. . . . Through the study of these collective transformational processes and through the understanding of alchemical symbolism I arrived at the central concept of my psychology: the process of individuation.[1]

Consider the following from *Alchemical Studies*: "The meeting between the narrowly delimited, but intensely clear, individual consciousness and the vast expanse of the collective unconscious is dangerous, because the unconscious has a decidedly disintegrating effect on consciousness."[2]

In the same section, Jung alluded to such a state of overwhelm as being a "schizophrenic process." In *Psychology and Alchemy*, Jung discussed such a process in terms of an "historical regression" and "splitting of the anima into many figures . . . equivalent to dissolution into an indefinite state, i.e., into the unconscious . . . (a process to be observed in its extreme form in schizophrenia)."[3] In the same text, he again describes this dark potential:

> The dread and resistance which every natural human being experiences when it comes to delving too deeply into himself is, at bottom, the fear of the journey to Hades. If it were only resistance that he felt, it would not be so bad. In actual fact, however, the psychic substratum, that dark realm of the unknown, exercises a fascinating attraction that threatens to become the more overpowering the further he penetrates into it. The psychological danger that arises here is the disintegration of personality . . . which may be functional or . . . a real schizophrenia.[4]

In the above excerpts, Jung referred to not only the process of schizophrenia itself but the feelings we have about it; that latter is the realm of the schizophrenia complex.

What we call schizophrenia could be described as the immersion of the ego in the unconscious, a form of dissolution. This corresponds to the alchemical stage of *solutio*.

Edinger describes solutio this way:

> The operation of SOLUTIO is one of the major procedures in alchemy. One text says, "*Solutio* is the root of alchemy." In many places the whole *opus* is summarized by the phrase "Dissolve and coagulate." Just as *calcinatio* pertains to the element fire, *coagulatio* to the element earth, and *sublimatio* to the element air, so *solutio* pertains to water. Basically, *solutio* turns a solid into a liquid. The solid seems to disappear into the solvent as if it had been swallowed up. For the alchemist, *solutio* often meant the return of differentiated matter to its original undifferentiated state—that is, to *prima materia*. Water was thought of as the womb and *solutio* as a return to the womb for rebirth.[5]

Edinger suggested that this state of immersion in the undifferentiated waters (of the unconscious) is necessary for positive transformation and actually corresponds to the process of a successful therapy or analysis, which "examines the products of the unconscious and puts the established ego attitudes into question."[6] There are various ways in which this immersion in the unconscious can occur, the outcome of which depends largely upon the relative stability of the ego. One may undergo a figurative trial by dismemberment via descent into the unconscious, from which a fairly well-developed ego would subsequently emerge. Or one may undergo a blissful but dangerous process that fits Neumann's concept of uroboric incest, in which an immature ego might be engulfed.[7]

In order for things to work out in the aftermath of any form of psychic dissolution, a next stage of *coagulatio* must follow, whereby, Edinger said, "archetypal contents . . . are egoized."[8] In other words, according to Jung, the ego recovers sufficient consolidation to be central to the person's experience, which is then organized around it.[9] In therapy or analysis, this next stage is promoted by a good enough therapist or analyst. Edinger further stated,

> The extreme case of failure of the archetypal images to become concretized [in other words, when one is stuck in solutio] *is found in overt schizophrenia*. The ego is literally inundated by boundless, primordial, archetypal images. *Such an individual has had inadequate opportunity to experience the archetypes mediated and personalized through human relationships* [emphasis added].[10]

This last statement implies a strong psychological and developmental component to schizophrenia.

This statement is also loaded because it seems to suggest causality between the "opportunity" (or lack thereof) for effective interpersonal relationships and schizophrenia. This reasoning does not apply to everyone who suffers from the condition. What of the individual who has had such relationships, has had the opportunity for them—and then appears to lose the capacity to maintain them? Then the dissolution might be a sort of alchemical reversal: the apparent regression into solutio of contents that seemed to have successfully reached the stage of coagulatio.

Yet a descent into solutio from a stage of coagulatio may not be a reversal. It may be part of an ongoing cyclical process, even of individuation, a process that develops over a lifetime with innumerable iterations. Jung referred to the importance of dissolution of the persona for individuation, the process of becoming whole, one's true self. Such a stage represents a necessary breakdown of the commitment to collective ideals or old defensive patterns that mask deeper individuality. As Jung described the process:

> I regard the loss of balance as purposive, since it replaces a defective consciousness by the automatic and instinctive activity of the unconscious, which is aiming all the time at the creation of new balance and will moreover achieve this aim, provided that the conscious mind is capable of assimilating the contents produced by the unconscious, i.e., of understanding and digesting them.[11]

Thus, the state of disintegration, or solutio, may well lead to a state of chaos for the individual—that may then lead to a new state of coagulatio.

The way Edinger talked about the stages of solutio and coagulatio in schizophrenia is reductive, limiting, and linear. Sometimes those stages are neither sequential nor predictable. Jung referred to the stages of early development in terms of the child's psychic emergence from the unconscious, intermittently challenged by the world of the archetypes. A child with a growing, healthy ego develops the sense of a differentiated "I," separate from parents. Jung wrote:

In the childish stage of consciousness there are as yet no problems; nothing depends upon the subject, for the child itself is still fully dependent upon its parents. It is as though it were not yet completely born, but were still enclosed in the psychic atmosphere of its parents. Psychic birth, and with it the conscious differentiation from the parents, only takes place at puberty. . . . For most people it is the demands of life which harshly put an end to the dreams of childhood. If the individual is sufficiently well prepared, the transition to a profession or career can take place smoothly. But if he clings to illusions that are contrary to reality, then problems will surely arise.[12]

My son had periodic archetypal experiences consistent with a normal growing up and demonstrated the capacity to operate with healthy, emerging ego stability in response to these challenges; he was able to avoid "clinging to illusions that are contrary to reality." He had a sufficient relational container to allow him to integrate these developmental archetypal experiences—until his early twenties. Since his descent into solutio at that point in his life, now that he is in his mid-thirties he has a newfound sense of coagulatio.

I think it is a synchronicity—a meaningful coincidence—that the onset of what we call schizophrenia often coincides with the entry into young adulthood at the crucial juncture when real world demands for independence are intensified. Some individuals enter young adulthood with a well-enough-developed ego and balanced enough ego-Self relationship to navigate the flood of archetypal contents that accompany this crucial milestone. Then there are those for whom the balance is off, leaving them inadequately prepared. Such an individual then "clings to illusions that are contrary to reality," as Jung stated, and "problems will surely arise." Perhaps the containing parental frame has been insufficient. Or perhaps they have experienced the opposite: a too-comfortable nest.

Faced with an inevitable crossroads, each individual's experience represents a unique confluence of factors. These include not only environmental circumstances (such as stress) and relational and family history, but also sensitivity, character, personality, biology—and timing. Due to the synergistic influence of these inner and outer factors at the brink of adulthood, an individual may be ill equipped to handle the challenge of any ego-conscious choice toward maturation in the real world with equanimity. Readiness is key. The lure of the imaginal realm of childhood must be navigated to allow a working relationship between fantasy and reality, between the conscious and unconscious dimensions of our existence, in order to move forward into the next phase of maturation.

At least psychologically, emotionally, and perhaps spiritually, the processes of solutio and coagulatio happen not only once but repeatedly throughout a lifetime. This may be why we revisit the same issues at different stages of our lives. Given this perspective, a schizophrenic experience of solutio might not be a failure as much as an indication that yet another coagulatio is needed.

This more cyclical perspective allows the possibility that people with schizophrenia can get better, which flies against every theory about it within mainstream psychiatry. Recently, a psychiatrist friend visited our office, where my son was working. My son greeted him and was his usual, sweet self; he has always had good social skills. They had a pleasant interchange with direct-eye contact, witnessed by my husband. This friend had known all of us for many years before, during, and after my son's journey into the depths. After this encounter, our psychiatrist friend took my husband aside and told him, "There's no way he has schizophrenia." He formed this conclusion because, from his perspective, my son had gotten better. That both could be true was inconceivable.

In therapy or analysis, absent psychosis there can be a solutio because the puzzle pieces of ego and personality may (or even need to) fall apart before being reassembled differently. The fear that is constellated in response to schizophrenia is less about the rending asunder of outmoded ego and personality structures in the movement toward a new configuration, than it is about the directionless erosion of what appears to be an established development—into a state of solutio we assume is permanent. *With schizophrenia, dissolution is terrifying because we assume it must mean an irrevocable loss rather than a step in a growth process.*

While it is true that individuals with schizophrenia do sometimes get better, many do not, and some go back and forth between worlds—meaning that they are only intermittently accessible to the rest of us. Perhaps most gut wrenching about an encounter with this phenomenon is its unpredictability. Schizophrenia throws our ideas about maturational trajectory into a tailspin. Assuming the worst can feel preferable to the open-ended anxiety of facing the unknown, but that assumption about schizophrenia—that it is a permanent state of solutio— also contributes to the overwhelming emotional response to it that results in a complex. Part of what is intolerable about schizophrenia is the hopelessness it engenders. Our fear of having hope in the midst of uncertain circumstances is often greater than our willingness to settle for dire outcomes, which at least seem predictable. Hopelessness helps us avoid feeling out of control and risking disappointment.

In the realm of the schizophrenia complex, those closest to an afflicted individual may have shared a lifetime with them, experiencing their capacity for relationship and functioning in the outer world—only to be confronted with the emergence of a different reality altogether. At that turning point those others—parents, siblings, lovers, friends—inevitably grapple with unanswerable questions. Was this unforeseen turn of events somehow of their doing? Perhaps worse yet is the question, were their automatic, treasured presumptions about this individual and their relationship *real*? Even if so, clearly the cord was still not strong enough to hold them, which is a realization that brings its own sorrow. To love someone with schizophrenia can be terrifying and heartbreaking. One devastating impact of the condition is that it can defy the human relational capacity. How can one reach such an individual when the receptor sites are all under water? Trying is not only natural but may also be a recipe for disappointment, which becomes its own trauma. Thus, individuals with schizophrenia often carry with them a wagon train of others tethered to them, all yanked into the swirling waters of the schizophrenia complex together.

Edinger's alchemical allusions suggest that the process of psychic dissolution and coagulation is a human universal, maybe even necessary to an evolving ego. Perhaps that is one of the reasons we generally find any encounter with schizophrenia so terrifying: it eerily reminds us of a part of our human potential, our personal psychic landscape, even our destiny, that we would much prefer to avoid thinking about, let alone experiencing. As mentioned earlier, Jung said a complex is "the *image* of a certain psychic situation which is strongly accentuated emotionally and is, moreover, incompatible with the habitual attitude of consciousness."[13] What we call schizophrenia represents an emotionally loaded psychic reality that is incompatible with our habitually held conscious attitude, so our response to the disturbing image can become a complex. Schizophrenia is an enactment of a state of solutio, of chaos unregulated, of an ego flooded with unconscious contents. Encountering that reality can throw us off balance, and make us frightened and unable to assimilate or understand. Such ego-dystonic thoughts and feelings are likely to form a schizophrenia complex.

Schizophrenia, the Role of Affect, and Mythology

The dynamic interchange between chaos and order is fundamental to what we call schizophrenia, as well as the emotions constellated by an encounter with the phenomenon. The archetypal theme of the interplay between chaos and order is frequently depicted in world mythology in a variety of ways spanning time and culture. I will draw out but a few threads from the vast tapestry of mythologies relevant to this theme. If chaos represents the state of schizophrenia, then order corresponds to the ego consolidation necessary to restabilize. Our emotional responses to order are usually ego syntonic; not so to chaos. Chaos is usually experienced as threatening. When the level of threat is felt to be intolerable, it is likely to go into a complex.

Icarus

One myth from ancient Greece containing these disparate elements is the classic story of Icarus. His father is the master craftsman, Daedalus, creator of the labyrinth. Icarus and his father attempt to escape from Crete using wings Daedalus has constructed from feathers and wax. Daedalus warns Icarus not to fly either too low or too high, lest the sea's dampness clog the wings or the sun's heat melt them. But Icarus does fly too close to the sun, his wings melt, and he tumbles from the sky into the ocean, where he drowns. This image is an archetypal backdrop for the story of schizophrenia.

The myth of Icarus can be construed as a warning against complacency or insufficient libido (flying too low) or hubris (flying too high), but it also suggests what can happen when affect goes unregulated. Metaphorically, the wax holding our wings together melts and we can no longer keep on course and steer. We lose navigation of our lives. As an archetypal image, the sun can represent enlightenment, creativity, energy, and spiritual wisdom; but getting too close to it—becoming inflated and losing a balanced perspective—can burn and destroy. The capacity to regulate affect is compromised in schizophrenia; affect becomes disconnected from ego consciousness. Icarus learning to fly in the middle, not too low or too high, could be understood as a metaphor for finding the necessary balance between consciousness and unconsciousness. His tipping too high destroys his ability to navigate at all. This is a metaphor for the seductive exhilaration associated with madness. Icarus meets his ultimate destruction by drowning in the ocean—in other words, he plummets into the sea of the unconscious. We can imagine poor, grieving Daedalus would have been left with a schizophrenia complex, his affect laden with guilt, shame, frustration, and deep sorrow.

The Maenads

The ancient Greek maenads, the "raving ones," as mentioned earlier in the story of Pentheus, represent the epitome of affect gone wild. These female cult followers of Dionysus—the lusty god of vegetation, wine, and ecstasy—were the most significant members of the thiasus: the god's retinue. Draped in animal skins and crowned with wreaths of ivy, oak, or fir, the maenads were irresistibly drawn to accompany Dionysus on his travels. While the more peaceful of their typical rites included gathering grapes and making wine, they are probably best known for their frenzied rituals, including orgiastic dance and the wanton murder of forest animals.[1]

The mythic story of the maenads depicts the potential descent from feeling joyfully carefree into being overtaken by unregulated instincts and affect with disastrous consequences. The allure of wine, dance, and frivolous sexuality unfettered can slide out of control into a chaos of madness and murder. Such a loss of control over one's emotions or behavior characterizes being in a complex—or a psychosis, depending upon the degree of disconnection from ego consciousness.

One can imagine that those solid Greek citizens who were not followers or fans of Dionysus or the maenads were nonetheless intrigued by them. Pentheus is the extreme example of how such curiosity could backfire. Others undoubtedly witnessed the maenads from the sidelines without disastrous consequences, yet with emotional responses triggered. If we "dream it forward," we can imagine the onlookers' initial reactions of awe or envy of the revelry then shifting into fear and abhorrence when the rite became an orgy of sex and violence. That could generalize into a fear of all things wild: a form of the schizophrenia complex. Those ancient Greek bystanders peeking at the maenads are an archetypal image of people gawking at individuals with schizophrenia—compelled, afraid, defensive, and repulsed. Of course, this scene represents not only what happens out in the world in response to madness witnessed, but also in the inner landscape of our confrontation with our own ego-dystonic, mad propensities, our own chaotic, unconscious contents.

Like the maenads, an individual in a psychotic state may be aware of feeling free and unrestrained or filled with unprecedented energy. This is affect disconnected from the sobering gravity of ego consciousness. The deeper one goes into the archetypal realm of the unconscious, however, the more likely it is that the return to reality comes with a harsh jolt. There may be irreversible consequences for out-of-control conduct toward self or others, including but not limited to physical injury or problems with authorities and institutionalization or incarceration. As Jung stated, "In schizophrenia . . . reality has all but disappeared."[2] The deeper the descent, the harder it may be to return "home" literally and figuratively, both for such individuals and for their families and communities.

Tiamat and Marduk

The myth of Tiamat and Marduk is one of the great myths of all time—a classic Ur-myth. The *Enuma Elish* (also known as The Seven Tablets of Creation) is the ancient Mesopotamian creation myth. The story, perhaps the oldest in the world, concerns the birth of the gods and the creation of the universe and human beings. Our focus within this extremely complicated story is upon the theme of the Masculine (ego consciousness/Marduk) bringing order to the chaos of the dark Feminine (the undifferentiated, unconscious/Tiamat).

The story of the goddess Tiamat is a quintessential, original Great Mother myth of the Feminine. She is salty, bitter, and fierce—and she holds tremendous capacity for procreation and her own brand of generativity. After she destroys her own children to revenge the killing of her mate, Apsu, by their son, Tiamat summons the forces of chaos to create a huge brood of monsters that cling to her; it is a daunting image of the potential mayhem of the Feminine, of tremendous, unchecked affect. Marduk ultimately kills her and in so doing plants the seeds of civilization, albeit a patriarchal one, antidotal to Tiamat's unrestrained chaos.

Jung discussed this myth in *Symbols of Transformation* in the chapter entitled "Symbols of the Mother and of Rebirth." He emphasized the "fight with the nocturnal serpent" representing a needed conquest of the (engulfing) mother, which parallels the basic idea of containing chaos with order to allow civilized progress:

> Against the fearful hosts of Tiamat, the gods finally put up Marduk, the god of spring, who represents the victorious sun [often a symbol for ego consciousness]. . . . After Marduk had slain Tiamat, he sat down and planned the creation of the world [things begin to show potential to be organized]. . . . In this manner Marduk created the world from the mother . . . the killing of the mother dragon. . . . The world is created from the mother, i.e., with the libido that is withdrawn from her through the sacrifice, and through prevention of the regression that threatened to overcome the hero.[3]

If the "hero" represents a staunch, conscious ego, the regression that threatens it as Jung described it is framed as

91

the choking enmeshment of psychological incest. However, the perceived threat to the hero can also be interpreted in a more general way: being overwhelmed by the unconscious.

Tiamat is a perfect example of overwhelming, unregulated affect. Marduk's victory over her dramatizes a patriarchal value of repressing affect. In Marduk's worldview, anger seems to be valuable, ostensibly because it is aggressive and powerful. But vulnerable, relational emotions are unacceptable. I found myself concerned that these emotions are left out of the tale, which is particularly troubling given that Tiamat is female—albeit a dragonish female—and she is a mother who suffers tremendous loss: first she loses her mate when their son murders him, and then she loses her other children when she kills them in dragon-like, vengeful anger and produces a hive of eleven monsters in their stead.

Feeling compelled to read between the lines, I imagined that, in addition to out-of-control rage, Tiamat would likely have experienced a range of other strong emotions, including searing maternal heartbreak, guilt, regret, sorrow, and pain. If the story had included these feelings, I conjectured, we would see a fairer, more nuanced depiction of the Feminine. Upon reflection, I realized that this emotional response on my part could be construed as a visit from my schizophrenia complex. I wanted to humanize Tiamat's character because I could not stomach its utter darkness, its absence of Eros. My confrontation with this archetypal character reminded me of my own confrontation with madness in my son, which had made me palpably terrified of losing him. I remembered that I could not have survived that period of danger without Eros.

My response to Tiamat reminded me of that painful experience and of how it still lives inside me. Intellectually, I

92

know that Tiamat is an archetype, that in her raw form she is an image of Chaos. By definition, she torches order, structure, and boundaries. No one wants to confront her; even the gods are afraid. Marduk does not get caught in a schizophrenia complex in response to the chaos of Tiamat's intimidating madness. Marduk represents the type of courage and strength required to face her. He represents the corresponding image of the archetypal Masculine to Tiamat's archetypal Feminine, the order and ego consciousness necessary to withstand madness, continue to function, and build a surviving civilization.

Symbolically, one way to consider this myth is that it portrays the character qualities of masculine order (logic, ego consciousness) and feminine chaos (unregulated feeling, unconsciousness) as polarities. As pure extremes, order can be authoritarian and unfeeling, and feeling can be anarchic. At the time the myth was written, the point it made had cultural relevance to the development of Babylonian civilization. For our purposes in interpreting the theme of the story psychologically, what is missing is the possibility of a broad range of moderated affect in the context of a well-organized ego consciousness. That kind of integration is also missing in schizophrenia, which can be conceptualized as a relatively one-sided experience of chaos.

Jungian analyst and author Esther Harding referred to the Babylonian creation legend (the *Enuma Elish*) in great detail, emphasizing the various stages of maturation and the challenges to achieving authentic independence. In her discussion of the story of Tiamat and Marduk, she refers to Marduk as "a hero destined to be the forerunner of human consciousness."[4] She stated:

If we take Marduk to represent the emerging consciousness of man, [his emergence among the gods and extraordinary powers] would imply that the new-born psychic factor of consciousness threatens the unrestrained activity of the gods, who of course represent the instinctive drives of the psyche. . . . As one begins to develop a sense of self and to differentiate the "I" from the "not–I," one seizes a little of the power of the gods. The ego threatens their untrammeled sway. For the ego has a certain ability to choose. . . [it] can know its objective and has the will power to pursue it, and this is beyond the gods. . . . [As Tiamat prepared to battle Marduk,] the female aspect of primal chaos, the dark region of emotions, took up the fight against order. . . . Marduk, who is a hero because he is a son of the gods, is yet much nearer to human consciousness than the older gods. . . . Apparently the gods were not absolutely sure that the powers they had conferred upon Marduk would be sufficient in the epic struggle. . . [with] the terror her very presence inspired. . . . Tiamat brought *her* magic against Marduk's. . . . And our own fight against the engulfing power of the unconscious is just as fateful. For as soon as we challenge the supremacy of the unconscious it becomes disturbed and threatening; its chaotic character becomes more marked, just as Tiamat "became like a mad thing". . . . The urge to consciousness, strangely enough, arises out of the unconscious itself, and in our struggle the as-yet-unknown Self that, as it were, *wishes* to become conscious, is on our side. . . . Marduk was not going to let her use her greatest asset, the ability to escape and reform beyond his reach. This is a common characteristic of the battle tactics of the unconscious, for although the unborn Self "wishes" to become conscious, the unconscious as a whole resists consciousness. . . . Tiamat [is the] embodiment of unconscious instinct and emotionality. . . . Marduk took upon himself the responsibility for the destiny of the world. . . . Perhaps the more conscious among them [the gods] resolved never to allow the Tablet of Destinies to fall again into the hands of Chaos. . . . Here we can see the very beginnings of personal freedom, the sense of responsibility and, too, the beginnings of democracy.[5]

This is an elaborate myth with many versions and interpretations. Marduk brings order to the emotional chaos of Tiamat, order that is restrictive but ultimately proves necessary to develop the human race and civilization. This idea in the myth presents a relevant parallel to what we call schizophrenia: while in a psychotic state, the psychic and emotional chaos one suffers is unrestrained by ego-driven moderation or order. Organizing consciousness is needed to control the dysregulated affect and the unconscious implosion that occurs with schizophrenia so that a person can continue to function—so that life can go on in the real world for that individual.

Schizophrenia amounts to a condition of archetypal takeover. Jung's discovery of the mythic roots of the delusions of the solar phallus man (see ch. 4) exemplifies the presence of meaningful archetypal images in the visions of psychotic individuals. It was Jung who made the discovery and extrapolated the associations, not the patient himself. The patient carried and described the archetypal image but could not have understood or explained its meaning. While symbolic images are present in a psychotic state, there is insufficient mental and emotional organization to differentiate and translate their meaning. The role of dysregulated affect is paramount. In schizophrenia, the ego is typically submerged in a chaos of unconscious contents. This condition is like Tiamat running amok: chaos prevails. No metaphorical Marduk is available to impose the regulation and order that are needed to make meaning of the experience.

Our emotional responses to schizophrenia reflect our relationship with the unconscious and our concerns about our ability to regulate affect with some sort of ordered cognition. We are all challenged to find a balanced relationship with both our ego consciousness and the unconscious. Our wariness about encountering schizophrenia may manifest our wariness about our own capacity to self-regulate, our private doubts and fears about finding the necessary ordering within to marshal our own inner chaotic contents. All of those triggered emotions in response to such an encounter can become a schizophrenia complex.

Psychotropic Medication and Affect

Psychotropic medication is a primary tool to rein in the unmitigated affect and psychic dysregulation characteristic of schizophrenia. Medication builds a boundary that keeps contents of the archetypal world at bay. Any discussion about schizophrenia is incomplete without mentioning psychotropic medication. Theories about how to manage the condition have toggled between radically noninvasive (anti-medication) philosophical attitudes, such as those represented by Perry and Laing, and more traditional psychiatric approaches, from electroshock therapy to antipsychotics, as mentioned in chapter 6. As appealing as a more laissez-faire attitude may be theoretically and emotionally, when faced with the reality of someone in a psychotic state—and considering the dearth of truly restorative options—loftier ideals tend to be preempted by whatever works in the trenches.

Having been through what I have with my son, I cannot imagine approaching schizophrenia solely as Perry or Laing posited. Their ideas are refreshing and liberating, but having searched thoroughly, I found nowhere in the real world where it was possible to experiment safely with allowing the illness to run its course sans medication, in the interests of promoting its meaning as a creative adaptation and inviting higher consciousness. I think medication is necessary, although certainly not without drawbacks. I also think an archetypal perspective on what we call schizophrenia helps to reduce fear and encourages empathic intervention through a nuanced understanding, integrating the realities of science and philosophy.

To use an alchemical metaphor, antipsychotic medication definitely coagulates—but to a fault. In terms of the interplay between chaos and order as depicted in the *Enuma Elish* myth, unfortunately, we have not yet found a balance between Tiamat and Marduk when it comes to antipsychotic pharmaceutical intervention. Even the best antipsychotic drug treatments act as affect hammers if they work to reduce or eliminate psychotic symptoms at all, leaving the patient in a heart-rending catch-22. To quote my son:

> I can feel the subject of love but not the meaning. . . . I do feel love but I don't feel it to the full extent because of medication. Medication is a very strong component. Anhedonia [loss of pleasure] is the worst part [side effect], feeling nothing and not wanting to do anything, no excitement, no positives. Looking back, I remember enjoying food, coffee, drinking, eating—sensory pleasures. I can't feel it in my body. I had free feelings then [years ago, prior to medication] . . . I miss it in a way—and I don't. Not on meds I had more energy but I can't live in society. The dream world is fun, but I have to take medication. I enjoy having stability. The medication literally saves me. When I started taking medication, it kind of put up a barrier between me and the world. . . . It became

difficult to engage with people. Even to this day, I still struggle with gatherings. When I was off medication, I was a chatterbox to everyone I didn't know, but I was talking as if I was a chicken with my head cut off. I aim to please. When I'm in a situation where it's uncouth to be who I really am, I will behave, because I care about people and how they'll feel.

The prospect of utilizing antipsychotic medication presents a paradoxical dilemma. Getting someone to take medication initially is all but impossible, since a characteristic symptom of psychosis is the gut-level, firm conviction that they absolutely do not need help or intervention. The term describing this sense is *anosognosia*. Anosognosia, or "lack of insight," is a symptom of severe mental illness that impairs a person's ability to understand and perceive his or her illness. It is the single largest reason why people with schizophrenia or bipolar disorder refuse medications or do not seek treatment.[1]

In Jungian terms, the state of schizophrenia could be described as a problem with the relationship between the ego and the unconscious. Edinger described that relationship in terms of the ego-Self axis—the connection between these two relatively autonomous centers of psychic being. In *Ego and Archetype*, he included illustrations showing the various developmental stages of that relationship, from an ego engulfed in the Self to an ego completely emerged and separate from the Self. In normal psychic development, this is a cyclic or even spiral process that can ebb and flow over the course of a lifetime.[2] Edinger's illustrations of this process resonate for me about the process of schizophrenia less with reference to an axis or link but more in terms of the submergence of the ego. As the ego is flooded, its functional autonomy is dismantled. The ego's ability to process and regulate unconscious contents is lost. Being swept up in a flood of affect and psychic energy can be exhilarating. An objective view of this experience, as well as a conscious awareness of the fear it might generate, is unlikely to emerge from this archetypal sea until the waters are calm.

Perhaps even in the midst of a psychosis people can be aware on some level that there is another layer of reality they are insulated from and that this other layer will present the need for a harsh adjustment if they return to it—so, they understandably resist. Given such a set of circumstances, perhaps even staying "crazy" may represent a necessary unconscious defense for an ego too fragile to withstand the onslaught of reality, and this defense can further entrench resistance to medication. Once such people begin taking medication, it generally does mitigate the flood of affective and psychic material, but it also often takes with it some of the basic joy of living—and certainly the exhilaration. So, one might go from too much of a good thing to too little: from overwhelming affect to flatness. Too much Dionysus is dangerous, but do we really want to banish him completely? You get along with Dionysus when you know your limits.

Affect and stress are key factors in schizophrenia and in the schizophrenia complex. Without medication, regulating the runaway affect of someone with schizophrenia is usually impossible. Medication can make it possible for the person to regain enough stability to function in the world, even meaningfully and with varying degrees of independence. But the struggle to find the right relationship with affect, ego, and unconscious remains an ongoing battle between the metaphorical inner and outer forces of chaos and order—echoes of the archetypal interaction between Tiamat and Marduk.

Stress affects everyone in kind, but for those with schizophrenia the degree of sensitivity and reactivity can be disproportionately, extraordinarily intensified. An unmet need, a disruption of schedule, an unexpected demand, or a frustration or disappointment can create a devastating storm of anxiety and distress. One place this outcome can show up is at the workplace. For example, I know of a young man with schizophrenia who was able to stabilize enough to teach special education. He was good at it. It was calming work with a predictable, manageable routine. That he had schizophrenia was not obvious from his functioning in that capacity—until anything changed in terms of the routine or its demands. Then he could become completely regressed and incapacitated. I imagine the overlap between ego and unconscious in such individuals like a fragile membrane filled with water, too ready to burst.

Even under the influence of the heavy hammer of antipsychotic medication, when someone with schizophrenia encounters undue stress, the delicate balance between chaos and order can be destabilized. Although a functional level of ego consciousness can be regained, such individuals live with an ongoing awareness of their own psychic and affective fragility, warranting a special kind of hypervigilance—in itself a form of schizophrenia complex that brings its own challenges, apart from the actual symptoms of illness. Those closest to such an individual are inevitably aware of this dynamic and experience an ongoing background condition of amplified alert. This ever-present background thrum characterizes their own schizophrenia complexes, often extending from worries about the loved one with schizophrenia to heightened awareness of their own psychic and affective vulnerability.

The Schizophrenia Complex
in a Fairy Tale:
The Three Billy Goats Gruff

Our responses to madness can be conceptualized in terms of how we respond to the interplay between chaos and order: the unruly world of the unconscious juxtaposed with organizing ego consciousness. Of everything I have witnessed and undergone with my son, what emerges centrally is the overriding importance of a strong, developed core ego in navigating the chaos of schizophrenia—and the glaring difference when the ego is flooded. Being with him while he was in the throes of his journey into the unconscious was like trying to hold on to a rudderless boat pulled by strong tides. Ego consolidation is fundamentally prerequisite to compensate for the psychic chaos that characterizes schizophrenia. As previously noted, Daryl Sharp wrote that "Jung believed that many psychoses, and particularly schizophrenia, were psychogenic, resulting from an *abaissement du niveau mental* [French. a lowering of consciousness] and *an ego too weak to resist the onslaught of unconscious contents*" [emphasis added].[1]

I have chosen the classic fairy tale, *The Three Billy Goats Gruff,* to illustrate the development of ego consolidation: a vitally relevant component of what we call schizophrenia and the complex it triggers. For someone with schizophrenia, ego consolidation holds the key to restoring balance. For those impacted by madness in a loved one, it is the primary source of strength and grounding that can provide healing perspective and depotentiate the complex triggered by such a close encounter with chaos.

The Three Billy Goats Gruff has been interpreted in the realm of children's moral education from the perspective of the troll (along the lines of "Don't be greedy"). However, while writing this book, I heard the story discussed by three Jungian analysts on the podcast, This Jungian Life, and perceived a meaning that synchronistically reflected my frame of mind at the time.[2] I began thinking of the theme of the fairy tale in terms of stages of ego development in the face of threatening unconscious contents. From that perspective, the authority of the biggest goat represents a triumph of ego mastery over the forces of darkness, avoiding potential splitting (separation of the three goats) and being devoured by the unconscious (the hungry troll living in the stream). Here is the tale as introduced and told by Linda Watts in the Encyclopedia of American Folklore:

> Three Billy Goats Gruff is a Norwegian fairy tale. It has an "eat-me-when-I'm-fatter" plot. The heroes of the tale are three male goats who need to outsmart a ravenous troll in order to cross the bridge to their feeding ground. The classic Norwegian fairy tale introduces three male goats: a small one, a medium sized one, and a big one. They are sometimes identified as a youngster, father, and grandfather, but more often described

as brothers. In the story, there is almost no grass left for them to eat where they live, so they must cross a river to get to a meadow or hillside on the other side of a stream to eat and fatten themselves up. To do so, however, they must first cross a bridge under which lives a fearsome and hideous troll, who is so territorial that he eats anyone who tries to cross the bridge. The smallest billy goat is the first to cross and is stopped abruptly by the troll who threatens to "gobble him up!" However, the little goat convinces the troll to wait for his big brother to come across, because he is larger and would make for a more gratifying feast. The greedy troll agrees and lets the smallest goat cross. The medium-sized goat passes next. He is more cautious than his brother, but is also stopped by the troll and given the same threat. The second billy goat is allowed to cross as well after he tells the troll to wait for the biggest billy goat because he is the largest of the three and will make the best meal. The third billy goat gets on the bridge and is also stopped by the hungry troll, who threatens to devour him as well. However, the third billy goat is big enough to challenge the troll and knocks him off the bridge with his horns. The troll falls into the stream and is carried away by the current. From then on the bridge is safe, and all three goats are able to go to the rich fields around the summer farm in the hills, and they all live happily ever after.[3]

The troll under the bridge is a monstrous, foreign threat that lives in the water, the most common symbol for the unconscious. He is a symbolic personification of the potentially devouring aspects of the unconscious, the archetypal contents that reside there. Those contents unregulated threaten our safety and sanity, just as the troll left unchallenged threatens to eat the goats that pass by him. The fact that he lurks under a bridge is significant. This bridge can be perceived as the challenging pathway to development, the only way to get to the richer pasture necessary for growth—which inevitably involves some form of confrontation to traverse.

The fact that the protagonists are three in number is noteworthy. Jung recognized numbers as "symbols of the Self's coming to consciousness" with the first four numbers in particular symbolizing different "phases of the journey of the Self, different expressions of its transformation."[4] Jung referred often to the axiom of Maria, a precept in alchemy: "One becomes two, two becomes three, and out of the third becomes the one as the fourth."[5] Jung used the axiom of Maria as a metaphor for the whole process of individuation. One is the original state of unconscious wholeness; two signifies the conflict between opposites; three points to a potential resolution—the third is the transcendent function; and the fourth is a transformed state of consciousness, relatively whole and at peace.

In other words, to achieve a higher level of consciousness requires working to transform unity into duality, then holding the tension of these opposites until a third stage develops to shift the situation to a higher, resolving level. This sequence parallels the emergent functioning of the three goats in the tale. In alchemy, the third stage is still incomplete but points toward resolving insight and the Self, the inner archetype of wholeness. Odd numbers are dynamic; they seek resolution in an even number.[6] The story of the three billy goats is prospective; it represents stages of development toward ego consciousness and wholeness. It also represents the transformation of chaos into order. The troll on the bridge over swirling waters blocks entry to the fecund other pasture. He is finally adequately confronted and swept downstream, allowing our three protagonists to remain safely united in the orderly, peaceful, nurturing environment where they can grow. In dealing with psychosis and its ramifications, enough ego consolidation allows a necessary confrontation with the dark forces of the chaotic unconscious for life to go on.

It is significant that our protagonists are imaged as goats. Animals in fairy tales often represent encounters with our deepest, visceral instinctual layers. That the main characters are animals intensifies the symbolic meaning of the story, since the tale and its message are clearly imaginary and representative rather than literal. These particular billy goats are usually associated with wiliness. However, according to *The Book of Symbols* authored by the Archive for Research in Archetypal Symbolism (ARAS), the goat as an archetypal image is a powerful symbol, universally linked with fertility or potent virility.[7] As such, goats can be seen as symbolizing life potential and generativity—and much more. *The Book of Symbols* includes the following passage:

> Unlike its cousin, the cooperative sheep, the goat
> is cunning and intelligent . . . hard to contain,
> feisty and temperamental . . . independent and
> . . . capricious. . . . Many of their rowdy and
> otherworldly qualities, including their ability to
> leap as if to fly, have associated the goat with
> darkness and untamed passions, yet this wild

ruminant has become one of the most nurturing of domesticated animals. . . . In Norse mythology this extends to the mystical ability to regenerate. . . . The Norse tradition also associates the goat with protectiveness as in the famous tale "Three Billy Goats Gruff". . . . Yet, the Judeo-Christian West has projected on the rutting billy goat's compulsive sexual drive and strong odor, together with its independence and strange look . . . the devil, typifying carnal lust and black magic. Upon the scapegoat in Judaic lore and elsewhere, sins, shame, or illness were magically transferred and it was then loosed in the wilderness. Psychological scapegoating defeats creative psychological growth, for the difficult conscious apprehension of shadows within fertilizes individuation and the ability to love, a wisdom reflected in the mythical image of the goat as the favored mount of the goddess Aphrodite. . . . The wild, lusty and independent billy goat was the inspiration for the Greek figure of Pan, the lecherous [half-human, half-goat] god [often joining Dionysus] . . . who compels untamed earthly passions and stirs insatiable desires and panic in the wilderness of the mind.[8]

The goat is both coarse and lustful, gentle and graceful. He is mystical and domesticated, fertile and potentially evil. The form of evil attributed to the goat is out of control and carnal, as in the reference to Pan. That characteristic coexists with the goat's potential for protectiveness and nurturing. As such, the goat is an image of the opposites inherent in human nature. The goat is thus a fitting protagonist for a tale about mobilizing all that we are in order to confront head on the threat of potentially devouring chaos and the drowning waters of the unconscious.

In this fairy tale, the three goats range from least to most developed in terms of their strength and power to face the threat of the troll. This symbolically corresponds to the significance of developing adequate ego consolidation to confront the chaos of psychosis. The first two encounters with the troll by the smallest and middle-sized goats are superficial, avoidant, tricksterish, and preliminary. These two smaller goats use their cunning to evade the danger (being eaten); and while they reach the desired pasture on the other side of the bridge, they do not combat the monster to get there, and they do not have their trio intact once they arrive. Viewed as aspects of one individual rather than three separate entities, the three goats might represent emerging stages of ego development that must be unified and consolidated to survive as an integrated personality.

By the time the third, biggest goat comes along, he does not need to outsmart or trick the troll because this goat can withstand the challenge posed by the troll directly. He simply butts the troll with his large horns and knocks him into the moving stream. Away floats the threat, leaving the bridge safe and the trio intact with plenty to eat, presumably for the long run. This third goat might represent an ego complex that is strong enough to confront and manage the potentially overwhelming surge of unconscious (archetypal) contents that inevitably accompanies various stages of developmental maturation. Such a surge certainly comes with schizophrenia.

With schizophrenia, the "biggest goat" of ego development does not arrive with sufficient strength to meet the challenge of the menacing "troll." To carry the analogy further, that biggest goat might be imagined butting the troll but falling into the swirling waters along with him. This means he would not only be swept off in the flood but would leave his two counterparts stranded in the pasture without his protection—as in a splintered ego. Imagining the scene forward, this image of the three goats failing to unify—two safely in the pasture but their third member, their protector, swept downstream—symbolizes the beginning of a psychotic break, when an individual's ego begins to split, to surrender to chaos. The individual is aware of being swept into an overwhelming current with enough ego consciousness to know they are endangered but not enough to fight the dissolution and find ground. Symbolically, this image can be interpreted as representing a schizophrenia complex with an associated feeling tone of disconnection, vulnerability, and chaos: a personality divided, rent asunder, and out of control. Witnessing someone we love metaphorically caught in the current is vicariously terrifying and engulfing. That potentially overwhelming affective experience—an archetypal fear of annihilation—can trigger a schizophrenia complex.

The Schizophrenia Complex
and Therapy

A depth approach to therapy ultimately involves working with the imagination. We humans do not live or sustain ourselves psychologically, spiritually, and emotionally by facts alone. Beyond the scope of theoretically based strategies for clinical practice, imagination is instrumental to any therapy or analysis— and most unequivocally when working with schizophrenia. The world of what we call schizophrenia is immersed in the imagination, in the mythopoetic realms of the unconscious. Clinical work with schizophrenic clients requires meeting them in that liminal space. Being genuine in such an encounter is uniquely demanding; it pulls at our own "mad parts." How we experience that pull as clinicians reflects our own schizophrenia complexes. My own ego's relationship with the unconscious is going to affect how I deal with a client experiencing psychosis. Work with the psychotic aspects of clients is both understandably repelling and absolutely endemic to a Jungian approach to therapy or analysis. Nathan Schwartz-Salant said:

> The tendency in analysis to sidestep the act of
> experiencing and embracing psychotic aspects

of a patient's personality is all too common. An analyst's desire to employ understanding and thus avoid the experience of emptiness and dissociative chaos is difficult to put aside. But Jung's psychology encourages us to do just that.[1]

Jung emphasized the potential value of meaningful therapeutic intervention with psychotic patients in the following excerpt from *The Psychogenesis of Mental Disease*:

> One should not underrate the disastrous shock which patients undergo when they find themselves assailed by the intrusion of strange contents which they are unable to integrate. The mere fact that they have such ideas isolates them from their fellow men and exposes them to an irresistible panic, which often marks the outbreak of the manifest psychosis. If, on the other hand, they meet with adequate understanding from their physician, they do not fall into a panic, because they are still understood by a human being and thus preserved from the disastrous shock of complete isolation.[2]

Cases of what we call schizophrenia differ vastly from one another. Clients who fall within the wide range of this diagnosis are as uniquely individual as any others. They differ in personality, function type, comorbid conditions, and circumstances. The common thread is their immersion in the unconscious. Since schizophrenia typically involves a loss of connection with the regulating power of ego consciousness, the relational demands of therapy can be extraordinarily difficult for both parties—depending upon the severity of disconnection. Some degree of a functioning ego consciousness would seem prerequisite for a client to be amenable to therapy. However, with these clients that may not always be a quantifiable or fixed criterion. Therapy may be as much or more influenced by the analyst's ability to participate in a non-egoic reality with the client as it is by the client's ego strength.

Remembering Jung's diagram of the analytical relationship (see p. 42), the unconscious aspects of both participants are also having a relationship in any therapeutic encounter. Entering a therapeutic connection with someone in a psychosis is *partly* up to the therapist or analyst, who must have some tolerance for his or her own chaotic depths to meet a client there. Whether the therapist holds an attitude of genuine acceptance in the shared field, or struggles with a schizophrenia complex, affects the capacity to be available to such a client. People with schizophrenia are often highly sensitive, with a heightened capacity to intuit whether they feel safe enough to risk interaction.

When we discuss how either the therapist or client feels *about* the condition of psychosis, we are in the realm of the schizophrenia complex, as I am using the term. If a client begins to become consciously aware of the "strange contents" with which they have been assailed, the response of the therapist is crucial to his or her adjustment. A therapist with a schizophrenia complex that evokes his or her visceral terror or rejection of such material—or even an intellectual defense against it—cannot provide a safe containing vessel for a schizophrenic client, even with good intentions. On the other hand, a therapist who can genuinely meet a schizophrenic client in the chaotic unconscious while maintaining a toehold on the shore (a courageous undertaking) paradoxically offers such a client an opportunity to take in more conscious reality. The therapeutic relationship then synergistically creates a shared field of mutual receptivity.

Working with schizophrenia ultimately challenges us to recall Jung's emphasis on learning theory well and then leaving it at the door in order to encounter each client as a unique soul. Consider the following from Jung: "As far as possible I let pure experience decide the therapeutic aims. . . . In psychotherapy it seems to me positively advisable for the doctor not to have too fixed an aim."[3] He added:

> Every psychotherapist not only has his own method, he himself is that method. . . . The great healing factor in psychotherapy is the doctor's personality. . . . It represents his performance at its highest and not a doctrinaire blueprint. Theories are to be avoided, except as mere auxiliaries. As soon as dogma is made out of them, it is evident that an inner doubt is being stifled.[4]

If the therapist *is* in fact "the method" of therapy, when working with psychotic clients the nature of the transference will depend upon one's relationship with one's own irrational core. From such a shared stance of not-knowing, a feeling of true connection may develop.

The therapist's narcissistic need to be in control, to prove his or her strategy right, and to fix the crazy "others"— even by loving them into conversion—will inevitably fail when treating individuals with what we call schizophrenia, because the ego consciousness prerequisite for such an approach to work is submerged in such clients. Rather, the therapeutic relationship requires a unique *participation mystique*, a soulful, demanding mystical participation. Again, from Schwartz-Salant:

> Speaking about a psychotic part is, in a sense, a contradiction. One never experiences psychotic states in another person as if they were a part of the person, as we sometimes speak of a complex. Psychotic states, like the waters of chaos in alchemy or in creation myths, are psychic spaces in which Cartesian language fails. These states readily extend to the analyst, creating a field in which it is not possible to state who is containing "the psychotic part." Rather, one deals with a field phenomenon that cannot be reduced to separable structures . . . not an approach in which one speaks of a "patient's psychotic part" as if it were in any manner totally separable from the same phenomenon in the analyst. Rather, transference psychosis constellates countertransference psychosis, but in a lesser degree and a more manageable form, that is, if the analysis of these areas is to be successful.[5]

Such a therapeutic attitude requires the challenging capacity to visit one's own psychotic parts enough to join the client—but in a "manageable form" in order for the work to progress. The therapist must metaphorically both hold the containing vessel and dive in. Any therapeutic experience is essentially unpredictable; with schizophrenia that uncertainty is amplified.

Faced with chaos and unconsciousness, a reliable guide to therapeutic practice based upon well-founded theory following academic research findings sounds particularly inviting and reassuring. Such an approach assuages our inevitable "inner doubts," as Jung suggested. In terms of actual clinical practice, however, while learning theories well is inarguably prerequisite, our capacity to respond to the unique needs of each individual client phenomenologically is nowhere more relevant—and precious—than when dealing with what we call schizophrenia in all of its many manifestations. According to Perry, "The most fragmented 'thought disorder' can become quite coherent and orderly within a few days if there is someone at hand to respond to it in a spirit of real, honest, and warm relatedness."[6] And according to my son in a 2020 email correspondence,

> I don't think that in the beginning . . . having schizophrenia there was any order or coherence within . . . therapy. I can remember having severe delusions and odd thoughts in the beginning of my illness, and in my opinion, no one would be able to give me coherence or order, because I sought the exact opposite. I didn't want to listen to anyone, unless they were giving me something of value, or helping me get what I wanted. . . . This illness if left untreated not only leads to all the symptoms but also includes a high degree of selfishness . . . and arrogance. When I was going through a major psychosis in 2015, I wouldn't have been able to talk to anyone because I was filled with fear, worry, and irrational thoughts that couldn't be tamed. . . . I needed a therapist first to

get me to open up my delusional beliefs and then . . . to support what goes against the delusions. Therapy in a psychosis can be very helpful if the groundwork being applied is logic based . . . [with] a therapist who will listen and interweave themselves cautiously to help the patient see a perspective that he or she was unaware of, and also including tips to help with certain triggers that induce the psychosis. If I feel that someone is afraid of me, I'm not available at all. They need to take the reins in the situation when I can't. It's very important to have a therapist that is caring and genuine. It enables me to have more trust in my words and be able to have a free flow of thinking. If a person is judgmental it makes me noncommunicative.

Effective therapy with schizophrenic clients inevitably involves toggling back and forth between shoring up an ego submerged in the unconscious and sensitively working on unconscious material as it emerges from the deep pool of the shared field. The varying theoretical perspectives discussed in chapters 4 and 5, including those of Jung, ego psychologists, and Laing and Perry, share a commonality despite their differences. They are less oriented toward a specific protocol or strategy for clinical practice than toward a philosophy or an attitude that informs the analyst's role in the interaction.

In terms of treatment process, an emphasis on spontaneously alternating between egoic and unconscious material with an attitude of acceptance and joining characterizes both the following case descriptions. Of the many encounters I have had with patients exhibiting schizophrenic symptoms over decades, I selected the following two to discuss here because each touched my heart in a unique way that resonates with my perception of the broader challenge of clinically working with what we call schizophrenia. These cases emphasize the crucial role of Eros, of quintessential relatedness—in this seemingly most unlikely setting for connections, the borderland with the unconscious.

Two Clinical Encounters

In both these cases, my focus became less on therapy that was curative or intentionally directed, and more on strengthening ego functioning. Rather, the primary focus emerged as the forging of an essential relational connection that helped these individuals feel less alienated and abandoned—as Perry suggested is ultimately most helpful with such clients. These are not case studies to exemplify the implementation of a particular theoretical stance or practice approach. They are stories of encounters. Each of them illustrates variations on the theme of the schizophrenia complex, bridging from the condition of schizophrenia to the emotions it can constellate. My encounters with each of these individuals—Julius and Jason—and their stories sparked different archetypal images in my imagination and stirred different feelings and emotions.

Through the lens of theories about key causal factors in schizophrenia posited by the ego psychologists of the mid-twentieth century (see ch. 5), while these two cases are quite different from each other in terms of background and symptoms, they share a relevant similarity. At an early age, Julius and Jason both suffered feelings of emotional and psychological desertion, especially by their mothers. In Julius's case, although he and his mother were always at least ostensibly close, perhaps overly so, she was intermittently radically rejecting. In Jason's case, he was adopted and never knew anything about his biological parents. Little is known about the specifics of the adoptive parents who reared him, but there was severe family dysfunction, neglect, and eventual abandonment. These two individuals could both be construed as having experienced emotional desertion and being pushed beyond coping capacity. Such a situation is consistent with ego-psychology theory about schizophrenia—that theory being that the condition developed when a child did not successfully connect with the opposite sex parent, primarily the mother.

In addition, both these individuals seemed to have generated a creative and adaptive response to a world that presented intolerable emotional and psychological circumstances, as Laing postulated about schizophrenia. Sadly, they did so with questionable degrees of overall success in the long run.

Such theoretical associations are all interesting. For our purposes, however, we will focus on the *stories* of these two unique individuals, Julius and Jason, and on their emotional valence in terms of their relevance to the schizophrenia complex: the thoughts and emotions constellated by an encounter with schizophrenia, for them and for those whose lives they touched.

Julius

Julius came to me for weekly therapy over a period of sixteen months about ten years ago. He was referred to treatment by federal probation. He had a diagnosis of paranoid schizophrenia, generalized anxiety with panic attacks, post-traumatic stress disorder (PTSD), and polysubstance dependence. He was a very tall, charismatic Hispanic/Caucasian, thirty-two years old. He was open with me about his psychotic symptoms soon after we met. He routinely experienced an auditory hallucination wherein he heard his personal information broadcasted. At the time he was initially seeing me, he was living with his mother, with whom he was both close and constantly conflicted. They had an enmeshed, charged attachment—a hostile dependency, full of mutual blame, adoration, and resentment. Along with a "hippie" lifestyle, she had drug problems while Julius was growing up. Having long been sober, she now appeared to be projecting her guilt onto him. She had introduced him to drugs when he was a young teen. Julius's father was not around.

Julius had been a wild young teenager. He used a lot of drugs, had many girlfriends and lots of sex, and generally was the life of the party. He was both lost and deeply under the influence of Dionysus during that period of his life, recklessly hedonistic. His school performance was mediocre when he attended, which was sporadically. He was bright intellectually but had attention problems and an unstable home life that affected his academic performance. At sixteen, his mother sent him away to a program called North Star out of state, a "tough love" wilderness program like others that were in vogue at the time for troubled youth. Julius described the program as a waking nightmare; the teens were emotionally and physically abused and starved. He witnessed one of his friends there dying from starvation and physical abuse. He felt the experience left him with lasting trauma, adding yet another layer to the painful, chaotic life events he had already suffered. He returned to his mother and shortly after she kicked him out again, all before he was eighteen. He lived over a 7/11 convenience store for a while. For about two years, he lived on a communal "blue hippie bus" traveling around California smoking marijuana, playing music, and making beads—a true

Puer, an adult man whose emotional life had remained fixed at an adolescent level.

Julius had a whirling potpourri of experiences in work and school, and he also had some real talents. He was passionately interested in cooking and attended culinary school in San Francisco. He worked as a restaurant chef and had a catering business. He worked for a bank and was in his very early twenties when he found himself in a high-pressure financial job. That was when he had what he described as his schizophrenic breakdown. He was using drugs, including methamphetamine. During this period, he and a friend robbed three banks. Julius described himself as the "polite robber." He always said "please" and "thank you" and never used a gun.

Julius landed in federal prison; his one-sidedly Dionysian approach to life had predictably backfired. While in custody he had therapy twice weekly, which he enjoyed. For him, prison may have represented the imposed provision of order he needed and had not found elsewhere. That was the first time he was handed a diagnosis of schizophrenia and also when he first began hearing his personal information broadcasted in his head three times a day, although this auditory hallucination was "better with meds." Maybe that voice in his head was a reminder to himself of his slipping identity. The voice came to him when he most needed to hold onto his ego consciousness, after his inner and outer world had turned to chaos. Like the smaller goats in *The Three Billy Goats Gruff*, this auditory hallucination might have represented his fragmented ego making a feeble attempt at asserting itself, a nonconfrontational reminder to re-member and survive.

I liked Julius. Our therapeutic relationship was readily established. The transference/countertransference relationship was easily maternal—my son was about his age; I was around his mother's. At that time, my son had not yet done his deep dive, but perhaps at an unconscious level there was a foreshadowing in the shared therapeutic field in terms of Julius's mental condition and my Great Mother countertransference. I yearned to "fix" him. Julius was more of a Trickster or a Puer than a Divine Child. His mercurial nature had served him well through his various escapades. My acceptance of him was not a deliberate strategy to build rapport or even trust. I felt for what he had been through and could see his strengths along with his tremendous problems, inner and outer.

He was on psychotropic medication at that time, and it helped to stabilize him somewhat but never altogether. His hallucinations became participants in our sessions. I could tell when he was receiving internal stimuli, and we gave it space in our dialogue. He could then acknowledge it and let me know when he could join me enough in our shared field to continue. We could sort through some of his delusional ideas together. We could imagine how he might get through events he anticipated would expose him to a high-stress environment or situation. From the start, Julius told me he felt he self-sabotaged; he would "try to go full circle but never quite complete the circle" and then would find himself "back to square one": an image of a frustrated uroboric process.

Julius was intermittently able to work, stay stable on his medication, and maintain some social relationships. Overall, he was cooperative with probation and less so with his mother's household rules. He missed a few therapy sessions but generally participated consistently during our time together.

My approach was phenomenological. I would consider the information that came to mind when Julius presented with certain problems or symptoms, but I consciously opted to allow the true subjective experience of our shared moments to inform the process rather than to impose what I thought he needed unless he let me know or showed me. I felt the breathing room was necessary for him—and for us—in terms of the pace, tone, and content of our sessions. It seemed he had been imposed upon more than enough. It spoke volumes to me that his primary hallucination was the broadcasting of his personal information; this young man had been violated and overexposed for a lifetime. He appeared to sense my acceptance of uncertainty and responded by becoming increasingly relaxed, disclosing, and trusting. Perhaps this is an example of what Schwartz-Salant alluded to—a shared field where the "mad parts" of each of us could float together—while I remained enough in control to experience my countertransference psychosis in a "manageable form" so that the work could progress.[7]

Within a couple of months of therapy, Julius reported he still heard voices and noises twice or so daily, as he had for the past six or seven years. When that happened, it triggered a sense of doom, signaling to him that tragedy or conflict was pending. It always took him from two to ten minutes to sort it out. He said that now, however, he knew it would pass, and he at least partially knew it was not real, even while it was happening. He described being able to control his reaction and turn it around when he heard the voices and noises at work. He said he was also better able to manage his anxiety.

We did a lot of bridging between his inner and outer experience. Julius had received cognitive behavioral therapy while incarcerated, but our process of validating, valuing, and giving full voice to his extremely busy inner life was different for him. Sometimes our focus was on delving into his unconscious through images, spontaneous active imagination, memories, and body awareness. Sometimes it was on coping strategies for daily life and ideas about a realistic future trajectory. We did deep-breathing exercises for his anxiety. We were creative.

Julius's inner world was so intermittently flooded with archetypal contents that our work together had to embrace and navigate that dimension fluidly, and not just in terms of his hallucinations. I think my holding awareness and acceptance of the archetypal in our immediate experience influenced what emerged naturally and spontaneously between us, often at the unconscious-to-unconscious layer, before emerging as a conscious expression in some form. For example, I will always remember us standing in my office facing each other while I taught him the yoga "tree pose." I did not deliberately select that particular pose; it just showed up. The tree is a vegetation image of such expansive portend, including but not limited to the Great Mother. Said Neumann, "The Great Earth Mother who brings forth all life from herself is eminently the mother of all vegetation. . . . The center of this vegetation symbolism is the tree."[8] Only upon reflection did I consider the synchronicity of the deeper symbolic association to that image as it pertained to Julius's archetypal story, which had much to do with the Great Mother—particularly as manifested in his personal mother experiences: the negative ones with his biological mother and the possibility of a safer maternal connection with me.

Regarding the schizophrenia complex, Julius did not have sufficient ego consolidation to have one. He could not fully access emotions *about* his condition; he was too preoccupied with his immediate experience of the flood of archetypal contents that engulfed him to gain the prerequisite objectivity—although he could communicate about his feelings and emotional responses in the moment.

I myself did not experience a schizophrenia complex as activated while with Julius, but years later what I went through with my son triggered visceral memories of Julius's condition, including the shred of recognition. At that time, in direct response to my son, I was bombarded with fear, sorrow, and nearly intolerable dread—and the concomitant urge to invoke my archetypal powers to fix (avoid) the situation. Overall, during the course of my therapeutic relationship with Julius, I was less identified with the Great Mother than with the positive, personal mother. My feelings and emotions were conscious and accessible, never potentially overwhelming, and I understood at a deep level that I had no archetypal power to fix him. The archetypal dimension to our work was ultimately expressed relationally. I think our relationship was the main reason Julius started to feel better. Eros was activated in our shared field.

In looking through Julius's file for this book, I found an envelope he gave me about a year into our work together. In it was a computer-typed page of his rather obscure poetry, but on the outside of the envelope he had hand scrawled in red ink the following: "A man who has not passed through the inferno of his passions has never overcome them.—Jung." At the time he wrote it, I think it was mostly a message from his unconscious to mine, which I received more consciously from the perspective of hindsight when I rediscovered it recently. The scrawled quote affirmed our shared resonance with Jung and Jung's ideas in our work together. That is to say, along with our ego-conscious therapeutic relationship we were meeting on that deepest level, unconscious to unconscious. The scrawled message had to do with his fraught confrontation with his own chaos. He let me into that chaos, and together we were working to help him gain a sense of ego mastery and order.

I knew not to expect a tidy therapeutic trajectory, but the way our work together ended is still sad to me. Several months into the second year of therapy with me, Julius suffered a knee injury that made it difficult for him to get to my office (or anywhere else). At that point, he was residing in a sober-living home. He somehow absconded from the residence without a word to anyone. The probation officer told me that the last time she saw him at the residence, he was behaving bizarrely and avoiding eye contact. I never heard from him again. I can only surmise that he slipped back into the waters of his inner world during a period of ego submergence perhaps triggered by outer circumstances, stressors, or substances. Nonetheless, I felt I had experienced a true glimpse of Julius, that there was genuine contact between us. That memory encourages me to hope he may have found a way to reenter the world, to re-member, and try again, somewhere. As is true about any encounter with the unpredictable chaos of schizophrenia itself, upon reflection it was hard for me to tolerate the unknowable about whatever happened with Julius.

In some ways this case was a therapeutic failure, certainly from an ego-conscious perspective. I offer it as an example of a case with someone suffering schizophrenia in part because of the way it evolved therapeutically, like a story right out of the unconscious: quirky and nonlinear. I am left to understand the meaning and value of what transpired in each moment we had, without a measurable, evidence-based treatment outcome. Nevertheless, I believe in the real connection we made despite the imperfect ending. I do feel I accompanied Julius for a while as he "passed through the inferno of his passions." I remain hopeful that our work together helped him to emerge from some of those flames and that he carries that healing experience with him. I know I do. I gauge my estimation of the quality and validity of our therapeutic relationship by knowing that I was genuinely impacted by Julius. In Jung's words:

> The relation between doctor and patient remains a personal one within the impersonal framework of professional treatment. By no device can the treatment be anything but the product of mutual influence, in which the whole being of the doctor as well as that of the patient plays a part. . . . In any effective psychological treatment, the doctor is bound to influence the patient; but this influence can only take place if the patient has a reciprocal influence on the doctor. You can exert no influence if you are not susceptible to influence.[9]

During my work with Julius, I could not have predicted the relevance it would turn out to have years later. I had no way of knowing I would draw from the unconscious well of that shared experience when my own son fell into the watery depths and I plummeted after him. The evolution of my therapeutic relationship with Julius in some ways foretold this later experience, less as a direct literal correlation than a symbolic one—a meaningful, relevant encounter I remembered like a whispered echo when I was feeling most alone facing my son's condition.

The veneration and love I felt with Julius in the transference were easily accessible to me, but powerfully present was also a dark side: his incapacity to sustain connection and the subsequent heartbreak of pouring so much into someone who then left, radically breaking the cord as though it had never existed. Upon reflection, the arc of my story with Julius included a prescient aspect that bridged from personal to archetypal and tapped into an essential content of the schizophrenia complex. The heartbreak of undone connections can be part of the schizophrenia complex and was part of mine: the universal human experience of abandonment. As therapists, it can be tempting to try to protect ourselves from unpredictable, shattering abandonment by using a broader intellectual perspective to avoid true heartbreak. As Julius's therapist, I suppose I sheltered myself somewhat in this regard from the full impact of his disappearance. As a mother, I had no such shelter as an option.

Jason

Jason was not my client, although he was enrolled for several years in the treatment program run by my husband and me about seven years ago. Jason was seen by one of our therapists who was my psychological assistant and whom I supervised weekly within that time period. In this supervising role, I was a deeply impacted participant observer. Jason, who had a clear case of schizophrenia, was in his late forties, Caucasian, and referred by parole. He had been arrested for the first time in his life for having urinated in public. He was subsequently convicted and briefly incarcerated, then released to treatment. While everyone in the office came to know who he was, I became aware of his case more intimately because of supervising his therapist. I have wrestled with myself about including him in this writing, mainly because he was not my client. Each time I decide not to, he shows up again in my mind's eye, so I must trust psyche. We always intended to commemorate him—through a staff training, a journal article, or some ceremony—but that intention was never realized. Maybe that is why he is showing up now from the deep pool of my imagination, as I contemplate how best to represent examples of encountering schizophrenia clinically from the perspective of the schizophrenia complex. Perhaps the compelling relevance of his story is in all the emotions conjured by this character. Despite Jason's ego submergence in the unconscious, his humanity moved many of us deeply. As the carrier of an archetypal image, he was surely our Orphan. This writing showed up as a fitting repository for his story.

At first glance, Jason appeared to be a quintessentially mentally-ill person, severely decompensated and probably transient, an anonymous huddle of limbs and apparel. In our waiting room, he seemed to sink into the well of his black clothing, a faintly disturbing nonentity. Sometimes he was not submerged in his clothing but sprawled half lying down face up with legs spread, or his entire body was curled too far over in the plastic chair, soundlessly mouthing scrambled words and obviously focused on a reality no one else could see. He appeared to be the kind of client that no one would be able to reach.

The first time I saw him in the waiting room, I went to contact Security; he looked like a deranged vagrant who had wandered in off the streets. I was advised that he was one of our clients. The odd contrast about him, as I quickly came to understand, was that as soon as he was recognized or spoken to, he would perk up and emerge so quickly it was startling, looking directly at whomever had addressed him with a pair of beautiful, sparkling blue eyes. He would then answer clearly and coherently—and politely. And, sometimes in the midst of one of his reveries, if he recognized a staff person coming through the waiting room he would suddenly snap out of whatever world he was in, say hello, and ask how they were doing. From the start it was evident that, along with being seriously disturbed, Jason was also seriously relational. That offbeat yet somehow holy image of the huddle of black clothing from which would emerge these startling blue eyes—this intact personality—is what I feel most compelled to share about this character. It was a metaphor in a moment each time it occurred.

In therapy, trust was built over an extended period between Jason and my psychological assistant. She grew to care about him deeply, and he became attached to her. The transference was clearly maternal, and her natural countertransference as his therapist was that of the loving, good-mother figure. He was so heart wrenching and needy and missing so much, right down to basic hygiene, that the struggle for my psychological assistant was to be the good-enough mother instead of dominating the shared field—and him—with potentially devouring, Great Mother zeal. We worked on respecting Jason's capacity for agency while helping him navigate his complicated and deeply troubled inner and outer life.

Jason constantly teetered in and out of chaos, intermittently out of reach. He never evinced sufficient ego consolidation to face the onslaught of his inner chaotic contents, let alone the outer world. To use our billy-goat analogy, he was always somewhere in between goats number one and two. Unlike those goats, however, he was not a manipulative trickster but had a guileless quality that concerned us all the more because he seemed so vulnerable. Our intuition proved accurate.

A key aspect of the therapeutic relationship was that his therapist genuinely accepted his inner reality, being nonjudgmental and unafraid in her responses. As she held this attitude, he opened up to her. They could talk about his hallucinations and delusions. They could alternate between his chaotic, subjective reality and the many challenges he faced in daily existence. Trust grew. With Jason, the fluctuations of the relationship between his ego and his unconscious were blatant and observable. He would emerge into ego consciousness and then sometimes suddenly, right before your eyes, the waters of his inner landscape would rise and he was figuratively gone—and then he would return. My psychological assistant told me that being with him was innately unpredictable, but she learned to identify when he would "fly out the window" right in the middle of a session. She learned to hold the space until he reentered it, and he always did. He cherished their time together, and so did she. I think Eros held them together, in some ways against all odds—as Eros is wont to do.

I have no way of knowing which pieces of his reported life story were factual and which may have emanated from the imaginal realm of his unconscious. In the end, I think it matters most that this was his personal history as he experienced it. He did not seem interested in deliberate deception. Jason reported having been adopted as a baby by a wealthy family in southern California. He never knew his birth parents. His adoptive parents were involved in the film industry, and his father kept a yacht in the marina. The parents had problems during his childhood, including substance abuse and neglect of him. Eventually, they divorced.

By the time Jason's psychotic symptoms—along with some substance abuse of his own—emerged in his late teens or early twenties, his mother was his only family, and she kicked him out. He never graduated from high school. He felt his family was ashamed of him. He spent years wandering the streets, in and out of shelters and motels, lost in his own world. While the narrative of purported wealth and associations with the film industry might represent an archetypal inflation, with him it seemed more a Puer-like fantasy if in fact it was not accurate, which it may have been. Mostly, he emanated the archetypal energy of the Orphan, alone, bereft, and forever mourning irreconcilable loss—of family, of love, and, in lucid moments, of his own sanity. That intermittent, lucid emotional experience might represent his own schizophrenia complex, his overwhelming grief about all his lost possibilities, the fleeting awareness of his radical severance from human connection.

Jason was completely estranged from his family and had not seen them for decades when we met him, but despite his psychosis and the passage of time, he had kept track of where he thought his mother lived. He would take the bus to the area and walk around, hoping to spot her. He never did. As he became attached to his therapist, he began to talk about his feelings of wanting to have a family and to connect with others but not knowing how. He suspected he scared people, but he knew he did not scare her.

Those moments when Jason was able to access emotions about how others responded to his oddness also suggest to me that he had a schizophrenia complex, along with the condition itself. In other words, he was not only troubled by his inner chaos but could be highly emotionally disturbed by how he perceived others regarding him. Occasionally, he could communicate about some of the emotions that constellated, which were barely accessible and nearly intolerable: rejection, isolation, shame, and sorrow.

The Great Mother archetypal energy manifested in Jason's experience with at least two opposite sets of personal mother figures. He had two negative, ultimately abandoning personal mothers: the birth mother who gave him up for adoption and his adoptive mother who cut him off. Decades later, his therapist provided a redeeming, positive maternal experience. In an interesting opposite mirroring of the double rejection by his negative personal mothers, I was a *second* positive personal-mother figure, an outer membrane of the therapeutic relationship between Jason and my psychological assistant. I was "there" in their shared space, figuratively holding the process between his therapist and him in a larger embrace. While deeply impacted by the turmoil of Jason's inner and outer circumstances, I think we managed to remain in touch with our true feelings and emotions about him without being swept into a schizophrenia complex. His therapist was able to offer a vessel that withstood his chaos and love him through it. That bond allowed him to begin to tolerate some of the painful feelings associated with all he began to re-member he had missed out on and to hope for change.

One of the ways Jason became well known to the office staff is that his therapist began to take him around and formally introduce him to them. He apparently had some social-skills training during his earlier life, perhaps in the purported movie-industry days of his childhood, because his manners were impeccable. He was even charming. For instance, he noticed when people wore their hair differently and would compliment them about it. Progress was slow. He and his therapist continued to spend time bridging his two worlds—his chaotic inner life and his fragile relationship to ego-conscious, outer experience—deliberately, gently, and diligently. She put him into a men's therapy group, where for the first time he had a positive, supportive, structured social experience with male peers. They were so welcoming and inclusive that he visibly glowed. During that period, the group had a Thanksgiving meal together, and Jason was a valued participant. He treasured that experience, unlike any he had before, as did his therapist. He had no family, and those men in the group were his only friends.

When Jason was to be released from his parole and subsequently terminated from mandated treatment, he wanted to stay in therapy. The therapist made arrangements with his parole officer to do a safety check on him at the residence where he was then living and encouraged Jason to continue to come to treatment voluntarily, pro bono. He told her he would. We all wondered if he would have the wherewithal to do so, left to his own devices.

As the weeks passed, Jason was missed around the office. His therapist was concerned. We heard nothing. Then one morning in October 2016, the local newspaper reported a fatal hit-and-run accident across town on the block where Jason had been living. The article was extremely brief. It said a fifty-four-year-old man dressed in black, walking the streets alone in the still, dark hours of early morning, had been struck by a pickup truck and dragged blocks to his death. The victim was later identified as our Jason. Our shock and sorrow were amplified by our shared symbolic image of him. His gruesome accidental death seemed a dark sacrifice of innocence and hope. His harsh demise represented the loss of this ephemeral individual, bearing archetypal implications; our Orphan was now forever estranged. His violent end of life symbolized lost prospects for reining in the chaos of his inner reality and entering this conscious one fully, despite his tenuous capacity for relatedness.

Jason's therapist and her colleague who had cofacilitated his therapy group visited the location where he had died. The story of his life and death touched us deeply in the aftermath of his physical presence: Eros prevailed in memory. As I have said, for weeks, then months, we tried to find some right way to commemorate him, but to no avail. The mourning has always felt incomplete, as though in some regard he had never existed even when he had been among us—an odd mirroring of the extent to which he lived in the noncorporeal unconscious that had now claimed him forever. It was as though he had appeared to us out of nowhere, alighted for earthly contact for a blessed stretch, and then just as quickly vanished.

When I write about him now, I still feel the twinge of dread, love, and sorrow associated with his memory. I still see his oddly beautiful face with the incredibly bright, light blue eyes, as he seemed literally to pop up from his mass of scrubby black clothing (that became cleaner over the course of therapy): a metaphorical enactment of the generative possibilities inherent in our darkest aspects. I remember his uncharacteristic, sprightly manner and unexpectedly adept social engagement as he began to be able to open up, to connect. His delight and clarity were all the more precious because they were so rare and fleeting, in such a contrast with the rest of him. Mostly, I remember the beauty of his intermittent emergence from his inner world, the feelings that were freed for him with his therapist, and the honor of actively witnessing that process. Sometimes a brief interlude is all we get. I hope that now this particular archetypal Orphan's story is duly immortalized.

My experience with Jason triggered a different manifestation of the schizophrenia complex than did my experience with Julius. Jason symbolically constellated a surge of strong emotions around the universal theme of innocent suffering: empathy, nurturing, caretaking. These feelings were readily amplified in response to him and were sometimes potentially engulfing, reminiscent of Great Mother energy; yet Jason also seemed to generate in others a kind of veneration of insanity. Perhaps because he was so childlike, our fears about his irrational propensities were far outweighed by our love. No one could bear to judge him harshly, in part because of what that would suggest about us—that we were unsympathetic, unfeeling, or even cruel, let alone fearful or avoidant—in our response to an orphan.

I suppose this response also meant that we suffered a degree of delusion about the whole of Jason's true nature— as an adult with a shadow and considerable life experience himself containing dark, unknown, and unpredictable aspects. That need to make him into a sort of outcast angel (the Orphan archetype) instead of a nuanced human being may have reflected limitations in our own capacity for true acceptance of people with schizophrenia in the failure to realize that their lives are just as complex as everyone else's. That incapacity also represents an inner split, which could be referred to as a schizophrenia complex as I define it here: our own fear and rigidity about the crazy aspects of ourselves. Our denial of those truths in ourselves went into the schizophrenia complex we developed about Jason. He was a psychospiritual manifestation of the bereft child who summoned our natural resonance with tragedy, some of which was at least marginally unbearable.

Clinical Reflections

Upon reflection, the feeling tone of my entire experience around the stories of Julius and Jason parallels what it feels like to work with schizophrenia generally. Ordinary rules do not apply. Clinical theories and well-founded philosophical insights aside, while therapy may facilitate a reasonable conscious flow of encounter and outcome on occasion, the nature of the process is skewed toward ultimate unpredictability. The role of psyche, of the unruly mysterious unconscious, remains paramount in any interaction with what we call schizophrenia. Such interactions are often intense, tapping into the human potential for destabilization and chaos, triggering deep fear and avoidance that can send us spinning into a schizophrenia complex.

Given the high degree of psychic sensitivity characteristic of those with schizophrenia, such individuals are affected more than most by the unconscious processes of any other with whom they are interacting. Thus, the nature of the transference, countertransference, projection, and introjection constellated by any therapeutic relationship involving the condition will be largely determined by this unconscious-to-unconscious layer of communication.

Psychoanalyst Harold Frederic Searles broadly developed this idea of the importance of the therapist's use of themselves in working with psychotic patients, recognizing the powerful interchange that was occurring between the unconscious of both therapist and client. In the mid-twentieth century, he was one of the pioneers of psychiatry specializing in psychoanalytic treatment of schizophrenia. His prolific work was largely ignored in the wider analytic community until the 1980s, when his radical views on the analyst's involvement through countertransference started to become more the norm. Since then, Jungians in particular have paid increasing attention to his work, linking his findings with those of Jung. Searles suggested that patients have an innate capacity to intuit the unconscious of the therapist and are strongly influenced by it. That radar is on ultra-high frequency in a client with schizophrenia. Searles said:

Schizophrenic experience and behavior consists, surprisingly frequently, in the patient's responding to other people's unconscious processes. . . The potential influence, for good or ill, of the therapist's personality upon the schizophrenic patient is even more awesome than that of the analyst in relation to the neurotic patient; hence it is especially incumbent upon the therapist to be as fully aware as possible of the processes at work in him and of their impact upon the patient.[10]

Perhaps the heightened sensitivity of someone with schizophrenia not only makes them more receptive to internalizing content from the therapist's unconscious but also more vulnerable to becoming overwhelmed. For such individuals, entering the ego-conscious world is a fragile undertaking, even through a well-meant, genuine therapeutic encounter. The case of Jason's "flying out the window" mid-session comes to mind. There may be only so much relationship these individuals can tolerate, in the sense of receiving a hug when one feels skinless. The process of strengthening the ego-conscious mind of such a client requires a delicate level of precision—and companioning—unlike other types of therapeutic challenges. As Jung wrote:

Therapy aims at strengthening the conscious mind, and whenever possible I try to rouse the patient to mental activity and get him to subdue the *massa confusa* of his mind with his own understanding, so that he can reach a vantage-point *au-dessus de la mêlée* [French. above the fray]. Nobody who ever had any wits is in danger of losing them in the process, though there are people who never knew till then what their wits are for. In such a situation, understanding acts like a life-saver. It integrates the unconscious, and gradually there comes into being a higher point of view where both conscious and unconscious are represented.[11]

Certainly, the extent to which therapists have explored and accepted their true feelings and associations regarding schizophrenia and have depotentiated their own schizophrenia complexes will be pivotal in enduring the work of therapy—for both parties. As stated earlier, as therapists our relationship with our own inner "mad parts," with the unconscious, has everything to do with how we confront the phenomenon of what we call schizophrenia in our culture, in our psyches, and certainly in our clients. In some ways, the necessary bridging from the unconscious to consciousness so fundamental to therapy with such individuals is a process in which the therapist must not only metaphorically hold the containing vessel but also leap into it along with the client. Ultimately and blessedly, such a dive has the potential to be mutually healing.

The Schizophrenia Complex:
Archetypal Roots and the Role of Eros

The archetypes of the collective unconscious are timeless and universal to human existence. Archetypal images represent and amplify various common life situations and themes across world cultures. They ultimately and expansively mirror our individual personal experience in all its uniqueness. This is true for someone with schizophrenia as well as for anyone else. The voices in the heads of those with schizophrenia often represent a more concrete psychological experience of the panoply of representative character images than we all typically experience in reverie and dreams. To quote my son:

> I wasn't aware that the thoughts I was having were abnormal. I just thought that it was fun and exciting and new. It all started around twenty-one, when I would have imaginary characters around me whom I would have an interplay with.

There is usually more than one such character in the hallucinations of people with schizophrenia, and there may well be a chorus of easily recognizable archetypal images, such as a Wise Old Man or

Woman, a Great Mother, a Devil, a Trickster, an Orphan, a Fool, or a Divine Child.

Jung's writings are replete with references to the connection between the archetypes of the collective unconscious and schizophrenia. Consider the following:

> The archetypal motifs of the unconscious are the psychic source . . . of delusional ideas (especially of the paranoid schizophrenic forms).[1]

> In schizophrenics . . . the collective contents of the unconscious predominate strongly in the form of mythological motifs.[2]

> When people lose their hold on the concrete values of life the unconscious contents become overwhelmingly real. Considered from the psychological standpoint, psychosis is a mental condition in which formerly unconscious elements take the place of reality.[3]

The difference between the relationship with these unconscious contents in those with schizophrenia and others, lies in the role of the ego complex. In someone without schizophrenia, unconscious feelings and emotions are potentially accessible to ego consciousness, where they can be negotiated. However, for someone *with* schizophrenia, the ego is flooded, overtaken with archetypal contents of the collective unconscious. In such a state, rather than there being an overlap in which unconscious contents are accessed, processed, and navigated by an incorporating, governing ego, there is no middle ground but only water. From

Jung: "With schizophrenics, the unconscious proves to be not only unmanageable and autonomous, but highly unsystematic, disordered, and even chaotic."[4]

In other words, someone with schizophrenia suffers incursions from the autonomic unconscious. That state does not produce feeling-toned complexes. However, the feelings and emotions constellated by a schizophrenic state of unavailability, of disconnection from relatedness, are certainly consciously perceived by others experiencing the psychotic individual, which can trigger a complex. Further, oftentimes individuals in a psychosis are not consistently lost to themselves and others but retain some awareness of their plight, both during their voyage and definitely when they land. Again, from Jung:

> One should not underrate the disastrous shock which patients undergo when they find themselves assailed by the intrusion of strange contents which they are unable to integrate. The mere fact that they have such ideas isolates them from their fellow men and exposes them to an irresistible panic.[5]

Those feelings of disastrous shock, isolation, and panic are in the realm of the schizophrenia complex.

Archetypes represent quintessential human experience. They have cohesive themes. They provide us larger-than-life images of conceptual patterns, ways to understand human behavior; as such, they contribute an ordering function to our lives and how we perceive them. Schizophrenia is ultimately an experience of immersion into the archetypal realms, but the archetypal stories in that experience are undifferentiated. The

143

overarching archetype representing schizophrenia is the universal human experience of encountering chaos. The myth of Tiamat and Marduk and the fairy tale of the *Three Billy Goats Gruff* describe the significance of a well-developed ego in confronting chaos.

Although chaos might be the hallmark archetypal image for what we call schizophrenia in general, on a personal level the emotional impact of encountering schizophrenia, whether in ourselves or others, is another matter. That emotional response, the schizophrenia complex, has an archetypal core with feeling-toned associations and themes that vary and may appear in more humanized images.

Individuals with schizophrenia are vastly different from each other. They are potentially influenced by or identified with archetypes as different as everything else about their personalities and lives, just as is true of those who are not psychotic. Others impacted by those individuals—whether family members or clients or strangers—may develop their own complexes in response, and are influenced by archetypes that represent their unique experiences with such an encounter. There is no one universal theme that characterizes the individual experience of dealing with schizophrenia, other than the undoing of whatever you thought your life story was before you encountered that chaos, either within yourself or in someone you love.

For me, archetypal images emerged that were representative of my own particular experience with my son, a version smaller and more personalized than the broad-sweep chaos of schizophrenia. The archetypes of the Great Mother and the Divine Child were highly activated and relevant in my personal experience. He was my first-born and only son. He was a beautiful, smart, healthy, and engaging baby, child, teenager, and young adult—the image of a true Divine Child. He had a charismatic and popular persona. He was the captain of his high-school basketball team. From his birth, I had strong ideas, vested hopes, and idealistic expectations about his future, most of which were corroborated by our daily reality. Sometimes, initially, it seemed as though my Divine Child had been abducted by fairies, leaving in his place a changeling. It took time to develop a life-changing realization: my Divine Child was not stolen, because that archetype was not the real son who belonged to me, anyway. More accurately, my identification with that archetypal image was dismantled, and the truth was revealed, leaving a real relationship that survived a storm.

The Divine Child archetype is not just about our children but about us: our precious, idealized image of their futurity, potential, and promise that corroborate our own longing for immortality. That idea of the dream future is a destiny we believe is ours, what we long for and count on. We want to rescue and manifest the Divine Child in *our* child. Children represent the future, symbolically and literally. Everything is going to be alright if they are okay, if the seeds we have planted grow.

The Great Mother archetype has a multitude of dimensions. The one that resonated most for me was the personification of "I've got this." She will *force* destiny to behave, to make the dream come true. When an unchosen reality radically disrupts our best laid plans, the collision wreaks havoc. Our imagined future has been irrevocably altered by the true present. The loss is shocking, devastating, disorienting. Archetypally, the telos is knocked askew, at least in terms of what we thought we knew, what we believed we had the power to make manifest. That Great Mother archetypal identification in me has been undone, hopefully forever differentiated from my humanized maternal love, which is just as strong but far more flexible—and significantly less confident.

I have come into a more expansive relationship with the meaning of the Great Mother archetype through my suffering. Now I can speak with some objectivity about being possessed by her with a perspective of humility—rather like having been expelled from a hot-air balloon. My tendency when identified with her was literally to enact that all-consuming archetypal energy on a personal level by assuming my experience of the archetype was somehow everyone's reality. Fundamental to the nature of an archetypal image is its versatility. We can all find our stories in the image somehow—or in the myth, for example—but although the archetype is universal, our experiences are deeply unique and personal. In our delight with recognizing our subjective experience in the archetypal frame, there is the potential to overextend. That is one way to describe being identified with an archetype: we find and lose ourselves simultaneously.

My way of thinking about the Great Mother archetype has evolved, as my tolerance for a more expanded understanding of my own life-sized experience has broadened. In addition to remembering what it was like to feel relatively all powerful, I can now consider radical disruption as another manifestation of that surge of affect: the dark side (chaos). A more complete image and understanding of the Great Mother archetype also includes the sorrowful one: she who is heartbroken, powerless, and suffering.

Schizophrenia is a deal breaker no one can argue with and win. Upon reflection, years after the volatile crises with my son, part of me wonders—painfully—if this radical disruption was not needed on some unconscious level to blast my well-laid plans that were never his. The archetypal Great Mother can be overwhelming, even to herself. Being identified with her is exhausting, not only for the host but also for her intended beneficiaries. In classic archetypal, alchemical form, the unavoidable death of an old order represents both an ending and a potential opportunity. From its ashes the phoenix of a new beginning may arise—not what we had in mind, but simply what is. The self-identified Great Mother may learn to be just good enough—a tempered, life-sized version of motherhood. The Divine Child may be freed to grow into who he truly is, an adult on his own terms who survived an unplanned journey of initiation through chaos and darkness. His fate is yet to be determined, but it is now guided by none other than his own unique telos.

My disidentification with the Divine Child and Great Mother archetypes is one way to describe the depotentiation of my own schizophrenia complex. The schizophrenia complex deeply affects families. We enter this new phase together, each in our own ways. In my case, schizophrenia in our midst dismantled not only my personal archetypal identification but our family's, entailing the unavoidable letting go of our unstated but idealized assumptions about how we were supposed to be, to look, and to turn out. The family ideas about that picture had to shift and adapt to a new reality, with new expectations and roles. To some extent, this is true of every family in terms of the ideals we hold about the future. Schizophrenia is but one huge example of the kinds of unanticipated reality that can disrupt our images of how things are supposed to be. The dismantling of our idealistic, ego-driven pictures of what development and success look like is archetypal—perhaps even necessary to individuation.

The first jolt to our family's psychic balance, our initial encounter with schizophrenia, left our foundational ideas of family sometimes buried whole, rendered beyond recognition or redemption by turns of events too unbelievable and far reaching to process. Now we are no longer stunned, in denial, or wracked by grief in any acute way. We have a recalibrated relationship with chaos, leaving us grounded differently, grateful we all survived. There is no quick fix, no magic about this phase of adjustment other than the potentially redeeming slow, steady drip of love— Eros ever present in the wings. The losses echo more softly and new possibilities continue to unfold, slowly and unpredictably.

Part of depotentiating the schizophrenia complex is recognizing that we just have to bear life's twists and turns, sometimes without understanding, without knowing the reasons why. Facing schizophrenia invokes all that we do not know and cannot explain, for which we have no sure cause or cure. Heroic tenacity in the face of the unknowable, even the intolerable, is a broader, archetypal theme interwoven with the story of our lives. Maybe our encounters with schizophrenia and its associated complexes represent an essential truth: life is what it is, not what we want, need, or hope it will be. Yet the sometimes-hidden gold of our tattered existence may lie in the very worst challenges we face. In a letter written days before his death in 1961, Jung made a comment about God that seems relevant here:

> To this day God is the name by which I designate all things which cross my willful path violently and recklessly, all things which upset my subjective views, plans and intentions and change the course of my life for better or worse.[6]

What we call schizophrenia represents an immersion of ego consciousness into the deep pool of the unconscious. If the schizophrenia complex is generated by our panic about all we cannot control or understand, perhaps the potential for healing lies in submitting to the will of that divine tumult to which Jung refers, realizing the potential for individuation therein.

In the face of devastating upset, in our inevitable encounters with those swipes of fate that cross us violently and recklessly, finding enough gold to persevere is ultimately a matter of faith, perspective, and attitude. Jung's quote suggests that such seemingly arbitrary, mysterious, and upsetting circumstances also express the Divine, requiring us to withstand the opposites inherent in our human existence. Eros, the archetypal capacity for relatedness, is also part of our divine inheritance, even necessary—and perhaps most—when logic fails. In the end, in some fundamental way—if we are to survive—it is Eros who can tip the scales, heal a wounded family tree, a dead dream, a broken heart.

In Greek mythology, the god Eros is the personification of love and relatedness, a cosmogonic force of nature. Psychologically, Eros holds the function of relationship. Love is what makes a parent swim out into the deep after a child who has been caught in the undertow. Eros fuels our devotion and profoundly unreasonable tenacity; love can overrule fear, shock, and sadness—all the emotional territory of the schizophrenia complex.

Concluding Remarks

The story of my journey—my family's journey—with my son is fundamental to this book. I hesitate to say it is all about him, but, in some sense, it is. The bare truth of the world is that at some level, the personal is always at the very core of our life experience, how we assemble and understand it—and why it matters. There is just such an expansive dimensionality in us all, spanning personal, professional, and collective. Upon reflection, we can construe the ever-present archetypal underpinnings of our human experience. Holding an attitude of *theoria*, of contemplative looking, reveals the ever-widening ripples of impact generated by an encounter with what we call schizophrenia. Our understanding of the schizophrenia complex can impact us in a myriad of ways, from enriching our inner relationship with our own mad parts to making us more conscious of our emotional responses to such encounters with our family and clients and in our community. With increased consciousness comes the increased possibility of transformation and healing.

The schizophrenia complex is a response to the madness and irrationality that are an inevitable aspect of our human experience. The broadscale, archetypal theme of this complex is Chaos. The archetypal images that emerge in our individual experiences of the complex appear in less abstract, more humanized and personalized forms: the familiar characters of the Great Mother, Divine Child, Orphan, Trickster, Anima/Animus, Hero, and so on. Depotentiating this complex, as with all complexes, involves increasing consciousness around the denied or split-off material. The more we acknowledge and tolerate the mad parts of ourselves and others, the less possessed by the schizophrenia complex we can become in response to them. Accordingly, we will be better able to respond to what we call schizophrenia consciously, with curiosity, inclusion, and compassion.

I am no longer dominated by my schizophrenia complex as I understand my experience of it, although its contents remain part of my inner landscape, illuminated but never erased. I try to stay conscious of temptations from the archetypal realm. At least two are familiar: to overestimate the power of my loving care to fix everything and to overinvest in the specifics of my adult children's life trajectories. I recognize both those tendencies as manifestations of my Great Mother version of a schizophrenia complex. Another potential manifestation is more recent and seductive: to over-normalize our adjusted relationship with schizophrenia in our midst into a revised, sentimental fiction about the way things are supposed to be, to look, and to turn out.

I now understand as never before that sometimes we simply have to submit to our irrational lives and face the reality of what life brings without our permission. To survive, we must drop our expectations and denial, follow where we can, wait when we cannot follow or fix, and stay as long as we are still breathing. We invoke Eros and hold onto love, treading water, one arm gripping the rim of the deep pool.

Afterword

As I readied myself to finally send this book out into the world, I was struck by fear, inner resistance, shame—and vulnerability. A whispered inner warning shook me to my core. What if I am invoking ancestral disapproval, carelessly violating some unspoken agreement? Closer to home in the present, I felt a sudden searing guilt about how the deeply personal layer of disclosure in this book might affect those I love who remain in the world along with me. At the risk of anthropomorphizing my inner daimon, might he be idealistic to a fault? Is my sudden hesitation poisonous fear leading to a regressive attitude—or healthy caution? Might my own form of defense and denial manifest through exaggerated acceptance of an unacceptable reality that belongs hidden? I began to suspect myself of engaging in clever rationalization to justify over-exposure and sentimentalizing the unresolvable, when perhaps hesitation is a better choice. Eros can inspire me but not necessarily protect me or my loved ones from the slings and arrows of our judgmental world.

In the final hour, my inner daimon, while relentless as always, at least had the grace to allow me a sobering reality check. I am sending this baby of mine—this book—out into our tattered world, but I admit my doubts to my audiences, both inner and outer. With deep regret, I must acknowledge that by disclosing some of the personal family history included in this book, I risk invoking the very stigma I intend to reduce. I make this difficult sacrifice consciously, hoping that ultimately the ends will justify the means. The reason for this book is to promote healing. I love and respect my family. I have to give the world this book from someplace deep in my soul, called by an inner daimon I did not solicit and know I cannot evade even if I try. May Eros guide the outcome.

> For you only feel yourself on the right road when the conflicts of duty seem to have resolved themselves, and you have become the victim of a decision made over your head or in defiance of the heart. From this we can see the numinous power of the self, which can hardly be experienced in any other way. For this reason, *the experience of the self is always a defeat for the ego.*
>
> C. G. Jung, v. 14, *Mysterium Coniunctionis,* p. 546

Notes

INTRODUCTION

1. Jung, *Structure and Dynamics of the Psyche*, 96.

2. Neumann, *The Great Mother*, 3.

3. Ibid., 310.

4. Ibid., 320.

5. Jung, *The Red Book,* 366.

6. Goethe, "The Holy Longing."

7. Maram, "Dialoguing with My Demon," 23.

8. American Psychiatric Association, *Diagnostic and Statistical Manual* (DSM-5-TR), 101–138.

9. Schwartz-Salant, "Jung, Madness, and Sexuality," 3.

10. Jung, The *Practice of Psychotherapy*, 88.

CHAPTER 1

1. Jung, *Psychogenesis of Mental Disease*, 235.

2. Ibid.

3. Jung, *Symbolic Life*, 167.

4. Sharp, *C. G. Jung Lexicon*, 109.

5. Jung, *Structure and Dynamics of the Psyche*, 96.

6. Ibid.

7. Shalit, *The Complex*, 68.

8. Ibid.

9. Ibid., 68–69.

10. Jung, *Structure and Dynamics of the Psyche*, 96.

11. Ibid., 312.

12. Jung, *Psychogenesis of Mental Disease*, 235, 236.

13. Jung, *Archetypes and the Collective Unconscious,* 98, 99.

14. Vaughan, *Detective Comics.*

15. Jung, *Psychological Types*, 425.

16. Barry Williams, speaking at the Inter-Regional Society of Jungian Analysts (IRSJA) seminar, Santa Fe, New Mexico, December 9, 2017.

17. Jung, *Practice of Psychotherapy*, 130.

CHAPTER 2

1. Jung, *Dream Analysis*, 304.

2. Jung, *Development of Personality,* 77.

3. Jung, *Practice of Psychotherapy*, 221.

CHAPTER 3

1. Jung, *The Red Book,* 347, 348.

2. See Rao and Wolf, *Euripides' The Bacchae*; Gildenhard and Zissos, *Ovid, Metamorphoses 3, 511–733.*

3. Jung, *Memories, Dreams, Reflections*, 174.

4. Filer, *Heartland*, 4–5.

5. Jung, *Two Essays*, 28, 29.

6. Ibid., 29.

CHAPTER 4

1. See Escamilla, *Bleuler, Jung, and the Creation of the Schizophrenias.*

2. See Jung, "Association, Dream, and Hysterical Symptom," in *Experimental Researches*, 353–407.

3. Jung, *Archetypes and the Collective Unconscious*, 50, 51.

4. Ibid., 51.

5. See Zeller, *The Dream*, 45.

6. Along with "Association, Dream, and Hysterical Symptom" (see n. 2), Jung's other article on the word association test was "Psychoanalysis and Association Experiments," *Experimental Researches*, 288–317.

7. "Association, Dream, and Hysterical Symptom," 406.

CHAPTER 5

1. Sato, "Renaming Schizophrenia: A Japanese Perspective," 53.

2. Padel, "Freudianism: Later Developments," 270–71.

3. Bettelheim, *Empty Fortress*, 68.

4. Cohen, "Freud's Baby."

5. Jung, *Dream Analysis*, 76.

6. Jung, *Symbolic Life*, 167.

7. Jung, *Psychogenesis of Mental Disease*, 156.

8. Laing, *Politics of Experience*, 129.

9. See Perry, *Trials of the Visionary Mind*.

10. Hippocrates, *Genuine Works* 2:344–45.

11. Oliver George, "The Intertwining of Romanticism and Science."

12. Ritter, "Study Hints at Biology of Schizophrenia." The study Ritter cites was led by Harvard Medical School researchers at the Broad Institute's Stanley Center for Psychiatric Research and Boston Children's Hospital.

13. Jung, *Mysterium Coniunctionis*, 546.

CHAPTER 6

1. Jung, *Memories, Dreams, Reflections*, 209.

2. Jung, *Alchemical Studies*, 29.

3. Jung, *Psychology and Alchemy*, 88.

4. Ibid., 336.

5. Edinger, *Anatomy*, 47.

6. Ibid., 48.

7. Neumann, *Origins*, 17.

8. Edinger, *Anatomy*, 98.

9. Jung, *Psychogenesis of Mental Disease*, 227.

10. Edinger, *Anatomy*, 99.

11. Jung, *Two Essays*, 162.

12. Jung, *Structure and Dynamics of the Psyche*, 390–92.

13. Ibid., 96.

CHAPTER 7

1. Graves, *New Larousse Encyclopedia of Mythology*, 167.

2. Jung, *Symbols of Transformation*, 140.

3. Ibid., 252–54.

4. Harding, *Parental Image*, 55.

5. Ibid, 55–71.

CHAPTER 8

1. See Amador, *I Am Not Sick, I Don't Need Help!*

2. Edinger, *Ego and Archetype*, 5.

CHAPTER 9

1. Sharp, *C. G. Jung Lexicon*, 109.

2. Lee, Marchiano, and Stewart, "Authority: Who's in Charge around Here?"

3. Watts, *Encyclopedia of American Folklore*, 383.

4. Sparks, *Valley of Diamonds*, 61, 62.

5. Jung, *Psychology and Alchemy*, 23.

6. Jung, *Practice of Psychotherapy*, 207.

7. Archive for Research in Archetypal Symbolism (ARAS), *Book of Symbols*, 318.

8. Ibid., 319–20.

CHAPTER 10

1. Schwartz-Salant, "Jung, Madness, and Sexuality," 3.

2. Jung, *Psychogenesis of Mental Disease*, 355.

3. Jung, *The Practice of Psychotherapy*, 41.

4. Ibid, 88.

5. Schwartz-Salant, "Jung, Madness, and Sexuality," 3.

6. Perry, *Trials*, 131.

7. Schwartz-Salant, "Jung, Madness, and Sexuality," 3.

8. Neumann, *The Great Mother*, 48.

9. Jung, *Practice of Psychotherapy*, 71.

10. Searles, *Collected Papers*, 192.

11. Jung, *Practice of Psychotherapy*, 270–71.

CHAPTER 11

1. Jung, *Symbolic Life*, 652.

2. Ibid, 483.

3. Jung, *Psychogenesis of Mental Disease*, 224.

4. Jung, *Symbolic Life*, 353.

5. Ibid, 355.

6. Jung, quoted in *Good Housekeeping Magazine*, December 1961; see also Edinger, *Ego and Archetype*, 101.

Bibliography

Amador, Xavier. *I Am Not Sick, I Don't Need Help!* New York: Vida Press, 2012.

American Psychiatric Association. *Diagnostic and Statistical Manual of Mental Disorders.* (DSM-5-TR). 5th ed. Text Revision (Washington, DC: American Psychiatric Association), 2022.

Archive for Research in Archetypal Symbolism (ARAS). *The Book of Symbols: Reflections on Archetypal Images.* Cologne: Taschen, 2010.

Atwood, George. *The Abyss of Madness.* New York/London: Routledge, Taylor & Francis, 2012.

Bettelheim, Bruno. *The Empty Fortress: Infantile Autism and the Birth of the Self.* New York: Free Press, 1967.

Bleuler, Eugen. "Dementia praecox oder die gruppe der schizophrenien." In Aschaffenburg, G. *Handbuch der Psychiatrie.* Leipzig: Deuticke,1911. Translated by Joseph Zinkin as *Dementia Praecox or the Group of Schizophrenias.* New York: International Universities Press, 1950.

Cohen, Dodd W. "Freud's Baby: Beyond Autoeroticism and Narcissism." *Journal of Psychoanalysis* 88, no. 4 (2007): 883–93.

Edinger, Edward. *Anatomy of the Psyche: Alchemical Symbolism in Psychotherapy.* Peru, IL: Open Court, 1994.

___. *Ego and Archetype.* Boulder, CO: Shambala, 1972.

Escamilla, Michael. *Bleuler, Jung, and the Creation of the Schizophrenias*. Einsiedeln: Daimon Verlag, 2016.

Filer, Nathan. *The Heartland: Finding and Losing Schizophrenia*. London: Faber & Faber, 2019.

George, Oliver. "The Intertwining of Romanticism and Science through Metaphor." February 23, 2017. *Harvard University*; https://green.harvard.edu/news/intertwining-romanticism-and-science-through-metaphor.

Gildenhard, Ingo and Andrew Zissos. *Ovid, Metamorphoses 3, 511–733: Latin Text* with Introduction, Commentary, Glossary of Terms, Vocabulary Aid and Study Questions. New York: Open Book, 2016.

Graves, Robert. *New Larousse Encyclopedia of Mythology*. London: Hamlyn, 1968.

Harding, Esther. *The Parental Image: Its Injury and Reconstruction; A Study in Analytical Psychology.* New York: G. P. Putnam's Sons, 1965.

Hippocrates. *The Genuine Works of Hippocrates: Translated from the Greek with a Preliminary Discourse and Annotations.* Translated by Francis Adams. 2 vols. New York: W. Wood, 1886.

Jung, C. G. *Alchemical Studies.* Edited by Gerhard Adler. Translated by R. F. C. Hull. Vol. 13 of *The Collected Works of C. G. Jung.* Princeton, NJ: Princeton University Press, 1967.

___. *The Archetypes and the Collective Unconscious.* Edited by Gerhard Adler. Translated by R. F. C. Hull. Vol. 9, pt. 1 of *The Collected Works of C. G Jung.* 2nd ed. Princeton, NJ: Princeton University Press, 1983.

___. "Association, Dream, and Hysterical Symptom." In *Experimental Researches, Including the Studies in Word Association.* Edited by Gerhard Adler. Translated by R. F.

C. Hull. Vol. 2 of *The Collected Works of C. G Jung*, 353–407. Princeton, NJ: Princeton University Press, 1973. First published 1906 in the *Journal für Psychologie und Neurologie*.

———. *The Development of Personality.* Edited by Gerhard Adler. Translated by R. F. C. Hull. Vol. 17 of *The Collected Works of C. G Jung*. 2nd ed. Princeton, NJ: Princeton University Press, 1954.

———. *Dream Analysis: Notes of the Seminar Given in 1928-30.* Princeton, NJ: Princeton University Press, 1984.

———. *Memories, Dreams, Reflections.* New York: Random House, 1963.

———. *Mysterium Coniunctionis.* Edited by Gerhard Adler. Translated by R. F. C. Hull. Vol. 14 of *The Collected Works of C. G Jung*. 2nd ed. Princeton, NJ: Princeton University Press, 1970.

———. *The Practice of Psychotherapy: Essays on the Psychology of Transference and Other Subjects.* Edited by Gerhard Adler. Translated by R. F. C. Hull. Vol. 16 of *The Collected Works of C. G Jung*. 2nd ed. Princeton, NJ: Princeton University Press, 1966.

———. "Psychoanalysis and Association Experiments." In *Experimental Researches, Including the Studies in Word Association.* Edited by Gerhard Adler. Translated by R. F. C. Hull. Vol. 2 of *The Collected Works of C. G Jung*, 288–317. Princeton, NJ: Princeton University Press, 1973. First published 1906 in the *Journal für Psychologie und Neurologie*.

———. Adler. Translated by R. F. C. Hull. Vol 3 of *The Collected Works of C. G. Jung*. Princeton, NJ: Princeton University Press, 1960.

___. *Psychological Types.* Edited by Gerhard Adler. Translated by R. F. C. Hull. Vol. 6 of *The Collected Works of C. G Jung.* 2nd ed. Princeton, NJ: Princeton University Press, 1974.

___. *Psychology and Alchemy.* Edited by Gerhard Adler. Translated by R. F. C. Hull. Vol. 12 of *The Collected Works of C. G Jung.* 2nd ed. Princeton, NJ: Princeton University Press, 1968.

___. *The Psychology of Dementia Praecox.* New York: Journal of Nervous and Mental Disease Publishing, 1909.

___. *The Red Book, Liber Novus: A Reader's Edition.* Edited by Sonu Shamdasani. Translated by Mark Kyburz, John Peck, and Sonu Shamdasani. New York/London: W. W. Norton, 2009.

___. *Structure and Dynamics of the Psyche.* Edited by Gerhard Adler. Translated by R. F. C. Hull. Vol. 8 of *The* Collected Works of C. G. Jung. 2nd ed. Princeton, NJ: Princeton University Press, 1981.

___. *The Symbolic Life: Miscellaneous Writings.* Edited by Gerhard Adler. Translated by R. F. C. Hull. Vol. 18 of *The Collected Works of C. G. Jung.* 2nd ed. Princeton, NJ: Princeton University Press, 1967.

___. *Symbols of Transformation.* Edited by Gerhard Adler. Translated by R. F. C. Hull. Vol. 5 of *The Collected Works of C. G. Jung.* 2nd ed. Princeton, NJ: Princeton University Press, 1976.

___. *Two Essays on Analytical Psychology.* Edited by Gerhard Adler. Translated by R. F. C. Hull. Vol. 7 of *The Collected Works of C. G. Jung.* 2nd ed. Princeton, NJ: Princeton University Press, 1966.

Laing, R. D. *The Divided Self.* New York: Pantheon, 1962.

___. *The Politics of Experience.* New York: Pantheon, 1967.

Lee, J., Marchiano, L., & Stewart, D. "Authority: Who's in Charge Around Here?" *This Jungian Life*. Episode 108. April 23, 2020; https://thisjungianlife.com/episode-108-authority-whos-in-charge-around-here/.

Maram, Eve. "Dialoguing with My Demon." *Psychological Perspectives* 59, no. 1 (March 2016): 23–29.

Neumann, Erich. *The Great Mother: An Analysis of the Archetype.* New York: Princeton University Press, 1963.

___. *The Origins and History of Consciousness.* New York: Princeton University Press, 1954.

Padel, John Hunter. "Freudianism: Later Developments." In *The Oxford Companion to the Mind.* Edited by Richard L. Gregory, 270–71. New York: Oxford University Press, 1987.

Perry, John Weir. *The Far Side of Madness.* Englewood Cliffs, NJ: Prentice Hall, 1974.

___. *The Heart of History: Individuality and Evolution.* Albany: State University of New York Press (SUNY), 1987.

___. *Roots of Renewal in Myth and Madness: The Meaning of Psychotic Episodes.* San Francisco/London: Jossey-Bass, 1976.

___. *The Self in Psychotic Process.* Dallas: Spring Publications, 1987.

___. *Trials of the Visionary Mind: Spiritual Emergency and the Renewal Process.* Albany: State University of New York (SUNY) Press, 1999.

Powers, Ron. *No One Cares About Crazy People: The Chaos and Heartbreak of Mental Health in America.* New York: Hachette, 2017.

Rao, Sirish and Gita Wolf. *Euripides' The Bacchae (Greek Tragedies Retold).* London: Oxford University Press, 2005.

Ritter, Malcolm. "Study Hints at Biology of Schizophrenia, May Aid Treatment." *Seattle Times*. New York: Associated Press, 2016.

Sato, Mitsumoto. "Renaming Schizophrenia: A Japanese Perspective." *World Psychiatry* 5, no. 1 (February 2006): 53–55.

Schwartz-Salant, Nathan. "Jung, Madness, and Sexuality." In *Mad Parts of Sane People in Analysis*. Edited by Murray Stein, 1–36. Wilmette, IL: Chiron, 1993.

Searles, Harold F. *Collected Papers on Schizophrenia and Related Subjects*. London: Karnac, 1986.

Shalit, Erel. *The Complex: Path of Transformation from Archetype to Ego*. Toronto: Inner City, 2002.

Sharp, Darryl. *C. G. Jung Lexicon: A Primer of Terms & Concepts*. Toronto: Inner City, 1991.

Sparks, Gary. *Valley of Diamonds: Adventures in Number and Time with Marie-Louise von Franz*. Toronto: Inner City, 2010.

Vaughan, Brian K. *Detective Comics* 1, no. 787. December 2003. *Wikiquote*. https://en.wikiquote.org/wiki/Batman_villains_(comics)#Mad_Hatter.

Watts, Linda. *Encyclopedia of American Folklore: Facts on File Library of American Literature*. New York: Facts on File, 2007.

Zeller, Max. *The Dream: The Vision of the Night*. Sheridan, WY: Fisher King, 1975.

Index

About the Author

Eve Maram is a clinical and forensic psychologist and a certified Jungian Analyst in private practice in Orange, California. She is a member of the Inter-Regional Society of Jungian Analysts (IRSJA) and the CG Jung Institute of Santa Fe, as well as the International Association for Analytical Psychology (IAAP).

CPSIA information can be obtained
at www.ICGtesting.com
Printed in the USA
BVHW051412160922
647222BV00005B/383